*Acclaim for* **Marjo**

# THE DREADED

"With a sense of universality Marjorie Spiegel unabashedly explains that we who are able to make choices and value judgments must do so with a oneness—to alleviate hurt and suffering, and oppression over the oppressed... *The Dreaded Comparison* should be placed in schoolrooms across the universe."
— **Gordon Parks**

"... eerie parallels between slavery and dominance over animals are well described in this provocative book. We know that slaves have been treated like animals; Spiegel asks us to consider why we treat animals like slaves."
— **California State Senator Tom Hayden**

"*The Dreaded Comparison* is essentially a consciousness-raising exercise..." — *The Women's Review of Books*

"[A] gem..." — *Choice*

"This book is all the more powerful for the testimony of slaves and descendants of slaves who have voiced their empathy strongly with the rest of oppressed creation."
— *The New Scientist*

"Marjorie Spiegel... has written a deeply provocative book."
— **David Brion Davis,**
**Sterling Professor of History, Yale University**

"[An] invaluable contribution... Marjorie Spiegel's extraordinary book, *The Dreaded Comparison*, with its judiciously chosen quotations and stunningly juxtaposed illustrations... packs a huge punch." — *The Boston Book Review*

"... Fascinating, and beautifully concise." —**James Merrill,**
**author of *The Changing Light at Sandover***

# THE DREADED COMPARISON
## HUMAN AND ANIMAL SLAVERY

MARJORIE SPIEGEL

MIRROR BOOKS

REVISED & EXPANDED EDITION

*The Dreaded Comparison: Human and Animal Slavery*
This revised and expanded edition is published by MIRROR BOOKS, the nonprofit
publishing division of I.D.E.A., THE INSTITUTE FOR THE DEVELOPMENT OF EARTH
AWARENESS.

Copyright © 1996 by Marjorie Spiegel & MIRROR BOOKS/I.D.E.A.
Foreword copyright © 1996 by Alice Walker & MIRROR BOOKS/I.D.E.A.
All rights reserved. Printed in the United States of America.
Prior editions copyright © 1988, 1989 by Marjorie Spiegel
99 98 97      5 4 3 2 1

MIRROR BOOKS
*div. of* I.D.E.A.
P.O. Box 124
Prince Street Station
New York, NY 10012
U.S.A.

Library of Congress Cataloging in Publication Data
Spiegel, Marjorie.
The dreaded comparison: human and animal slavery
Marjorie Spiegel with a foreword by Alice Walker. — Rev. and expanded ed.
Includes biographical references and index.
1. Animal rights. 2. Slavery—United States. I. Title.
HV4708.S63 1996                     96-2591
306.3'62'0973—dc20                   CIP

ISBN: 0-9624493-4-2 cloth
      0-9624493-3-4 paperback

Printed on chlorine-free, 100% post-consumer recycled paper
with vegetable-based inks.

# THE DREADED COMPARISON

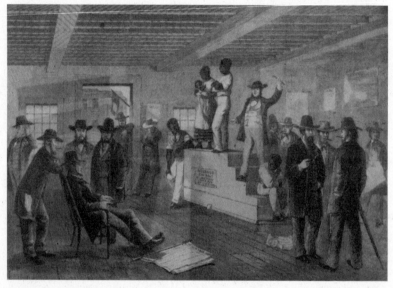

A slave auction in Virginia, 1861

The cattle market in Chicago, 1868

racism (rā' siz ᴇm), n. 1. a belief that human races have distinctive characteristics that determine their respective cultures, usually involving the idea that one's own race is superior and has the right to rule others. 2. a policy of enforcing such asserted right. 3. a system of government and society based upon it. —rac' ist, n., adj.

speciesism (spē' shēz iz ᴇm), n. 1. a belief that different species of animals are significantly different from one another in their capacities to feel pleasure and pain and live an autonomous existence, usually involving the idea that one's own species has the right to rule and use others. 2. a policy of enforcing such asserted right. 3. a system of government and society based upon it. —spe' cies ist, n., adj.

# SYMPATHY

I know what the caged bird feels, alas!
When the sun is bright on the upland slopes;
When the wind stirs soft through springing grass,
And the river flows like a stream of glass;
When the first bird sings and the first bud opes,
And the faint perfume from its chalice steals—
I know what the caged bird feels!

I know why the caged bird beats his wing
Till its blood is red on the cruel bars;
For he must fly back to his perch and cling
When he fain would be on the bough a-swing;
And a pain still throbs in the old, old scars
And they pulse again with a keener sting—
I know why he beats his wing!

I know why the caged bird sings, ah me,
When his wing is bruised and his bosom sore—
When he beats his bars and he would be free;
It is not a carol of joy or glee,
But a prayer that he sends from his heart's deep core,
But a plea, that upward to heaven he flings—
I know why the caged bird sings!

—Paul Laurence Dunbar, (1872-1906),
son of two runaway slaves

THE OWNER OF
A SLAVE DESTROYS
TWO FREEDOMS—
THAT OF HIS SLAVE
AND THAT OF HIM-
SELF.

—*John Bryant*

# CONTENTS

# FOREWORD
by Alice Walker

This powerful book, once read with comprehension, will take a lifetime to forget. In *The Dreaded Comparison*, Marjorie Spiegel illustrates the similarities between the enslavement of black people (and by implication other enslaved peoples) and the enslavement of animals, past and present. It is a comparison that, even for those of us who recognize its validity, is a difficult one to face. Especially so if we are the descendants of slaves. Or of slave owners. Or of both. Especially so if we are also responsible in some way for the present treatment of animals. Especially so if we, for instance, participate in or profit from animal research (what beings who loved life died for our lipstick, lotions, medicines and so on?) or if we own animals or eat animals or if we are content to know that animals are shut up "safely" in zoos. In short, if we are complicit in their enslavement and destruction, which is to say if we are, at this juncture in history, master.

But there is hope following close behind the initial despair that one feels on reading this book. Despair because one realizes one has eaten eggs produced by mutilated (de-beaked) beings crammed four to a cage the size of a record album cover; one has tasted veal from a baby calf ripped from its mother's womb without so much as a goodbye lick or look from her; one has used cosmetics derived from "products" forced out of animals' bodies in great pain. (The civet cat, for one, is whipped in the face until it sweats the essence that is the foundation for many a sweet perfume.) We are guilty.

But this is only a first response. And normal. What we do with our heightened consciousness is the question. It is the author's clarity that produces hope. Her scholarship. Her assuredness in pointing out the "dreaded comparison" between the pain felt by humans who are abused and the pain felt by non-human animals who are abused, and recognizing it as the same pain.

The animals of the world exist for their own reasons. They were not made for humans any more than black people were made for whites or women for men. This is the essence of Ms. Spiegel's cogent, humane, and astute argument, and it is sound.

# An Historical Understanding

Pain is pain, whether it be inflicted on man or on beast;
and the creature who suffers it, whether man or beast,
being sensible to the misery of it, whilst it lasts, suffers
evil... The white man... can have no right, by virtue of his
color, to enslave and tyrannize over a black man... For the
same reason, a man can have no natural right to abuse and
torment a beast.

— Dr. Humphrey Primatt, 1776

[The tyranny of human over non-human animals] has
caused and today is still causing an amount of pain and
suffering that can only be compared with that which resulted
from the centuries of tyranny by white humans over black
humans. The struggle against this tyranny is a struggle as
important as any of the moral and social issues that have
been fought over in recent years.

— Peter Singer, 1974

Comparing speciesism with racism? At first
glance, many people might feel that it is insulting to compare
the suffering of non-human animals to that of humans. In fact,
in our society, comparison to an animal has come to be a slur.

Why is it an insult for anyone to be compared to an
animal? In many cultures, such a comparison was an honor. In
Native American cultures, for example, individuals adopted the
names of admired animals, and had spirit guides—in animal

form—who served both as teachers and escorts into the realms of the spirit world. Names such as Sitting Bull, Running Deer, and Hawkeye are familiar to us, expressive of the admiration Native Americans had for the animals with whom they shared both the earth and the afterlife. Native Americans, Ancient Egyptians, some African tribes, and many other ancient and aboriginal cultures the world over have worshiped various animals as gods or messengers to god. So how is it that we find ourselves in a time when comparison to a non-human animal has ceased to be an honor and is instead hurled as an insult?

By the time the New World was "discovered" and colonization began, Europeans had "subdued" most of the land which they had for centuries inhabited.[1] Europe's wildernesses were long-gone, replaced with a very "managed" countryside comprised of "English gardens," rolling hills where mighty forests had long ago stood, and relatively few stands of woods, often maintained as hunting grounds.

Understandably, it came as quite a shock to the British colonists' psyches when they encountered the unbridled and deeply forested North American wilderness. The white Puritan colonists measured "progress" and "civilization" in terms of (among other things) how far a people could distance themselves from Nature. "Countless diaries, addresses and memorials of the frontier period," writes historian Roderick Nash, attest to this in their representations of "the wilderness as an 'enemy' which had to be 'conquered', 'subdued', and 'vanquished' by a 'pioneer army'."[2] To the average colonist, explains Nash,

> wilderness... acquired significance as a dark and sinister symbol. [The pioneers] shared the long Western tradition of imagining wild country as a moral vacuum, a cursed and chaotic wasteland. As a consequence, frontiersmen

16

acutely sensed that they battled wild country not only for personal survival but in the name of nation, race and God. Civilizing the New World meant enlightening darkness, ordering chaos, and changing evil into good.[3]

Holding these beliefs, white Christians were convinced that it was virtually a moral obligation to conquer any people who were still living in harmony with the devil-ridden, moral wasteland of nature—as "savages," in their opinion. Paying no regard to the level of cultural sophistication or even to the general happiness of the people living within their native societies, the conquerors merely saw "heathens" while proceeding to destroy entire cultures, along with the ancient ecosystems which had long supported them.

In 1688, the idea of the "noble savage" was introduced by English playwright and novelist Aphra Behn in *Oroonoko*. The noble savage hated his fellow slaves because they were:

by Nature Slaves, poor wretched Rogues, fit to be used as Christian Tools; Dogs, treacherous and cowardly, fit for such Masters; and they wanted only but to be whipped into the knowledge of the Christian Gods, to be the vilest of all creeping things.[4]

The slave who had thus capitulated to his master personified the beliefs about nature and the denizens of the natural world held by the Christian conquerors, who maintained that they were serving God by whipping nature, animals, and black people into submission. And how convenient that they could obtain a slave work force while performing their sanctimonious acts. After all, there could exist no moral obligation towards any of those in league with the forces of chaos, darkness, or the devil.

In the above passage by Aphra Behn we also see sign of the trend towards using comparison to an animal as an insult: "dogs, treacherous and cowardly. . ." Centuries later, an excerpt from an essay by James Baldwin exemplifies the integral part which this comparison has come to play in blacks' consciousness as they continue to struggle for equality:

> The American triumph—in which the American tragedy has always been implicit—was to make Black people despise themselves. When I was little I despised myself; I did not know any better. And this meant, albeit unconsciously, or against my will, or in great pain, that I also despised my father. *And* my mother. *And* my brothers. *And* my sisters. Black people were killing each other every night out on Lenox Avenue, when I was growing up: and no one explained to them, or to me, that it was *intended* that they should; that they were penned where they were, like animals, in order that they should consider themselves no better than animals. Everything supported this sense of reality, nothing denied it; and so one was ready, when it came time to go to work, to be treated as a slave.[5]

All of this has a negative effect on the lives of human and non-human animals alike. As long as humans feel they are forced to defend their own rights and worth by placing someone beneath them, oppression will not end. This approach, at the very best, results only in an individual or group of people climbing up the ladder by pushing others down. There is evidence of this approach in the world today: racially motivated gang-wars among impoverished youth; in the United States, white working-class racist violence directed at working-class blacks, who suffer from the residual effects of slavery in the form of prejudice and job discrimination; in Britain, black youths attack Indian-owned businesses. It is unfortunately common that those who feel trapped within circumstances they feel powerless to change often quarrel among themselves, feeling even more powerless to impact those who actually make the laws, profit from the system, and exert great influence over economic opportunities.

But winding its way through the history of inequality within our culture has been another approach, which today grows ever stronger; its main tenet is that we cannot maintain that oppression is fine for some simply because they are not like us. Only through a rejection of violence and oppression *themselves* will we ever find a long-term "freedom and justice *for all.*" It is not an "either-or" situation; the idea that one group will have its rights protected or respected only after another "more important" group is totally comfortable is finally being widely recognized as a delay tactic used by those resisting change. Women were told to keep waiting for years for their right to vote because other issues were "more important." Black people in the United States were told that their slavery was an "economic necessity" to be continued for the good of the country. Until the reforms of the early 1990's, blacks in South Africa were still being told that apartheid was necessary. Necessary for whom? Surely not the people who were living under this form of slavery.

With the exception of those who still cling—either overtly or subtly—to racist thought, most members of our society have reached the conclusion that it was and is wrong to treat blacks "like animals." But with regard to the animals themselves, most still feel that it is acceptable to treat them, to some degree or another, in exactly this same manner; to treat them, as we say, "like animals." That is, we have decided that treatment which is wholly unacceptable when received by a human being is in fact the *proper* manner in which to treat a non-human animal.

A line was arbitrarily drawn between white people and black people, a division which has since been rejected. But what of the line which has been drawn between human and non-human animals? We often behave as if there were a wide and bridgeless chasm, with humans on one side and all the rest of the animals on the other. Even our terminology reflects this attitude: we speak of "humans" in one breath, and in the next, lump all other animals into one grab-bag of a category entitled "non-human animals." On what basis was this line drawn? Surely the line, if it need be drawn at all, could have been placed with equal or greater accuracy in any one of a number of places. We are, for instance, much closer genetically and behaviorally to other primates than non-human primates are to toads. So perhaps the line could be drawn *after* other primates. Or, the line could just as reasonably be drawn so as to separate all mammals from other creatures, for mammals share common attributes which other animals lack.

But one problem with this approach is that it presupposes some sort of "worst-to-best" ascension list, ranging from the "simplest" beings straight up to human beings—at the top, of course. This attempt to rank species reflects a chronic misinterpretation and misapplication of Darwin's evolutionary theory, falsely concluding that humans are evolution's "finished product." On the contrary, Darwin's *Origin Of Species* implied that humans were evolutionary first cousins to modern-day apes and orangutans, all distinctly and simultaneously evolving from a common ancestor, just as, for example, distinct species of cats branched off from an ancient feline form. Darwin went further, writing in his notebook that "animals may partake from our common origin in one ancestor. . . we may all be netted together."

Darwin was even more specific in his views about the commonalities between other animals and the human species.

"The senses and intuitions," wrote Darwin in 1871, "the various emotions and faculties, such as love, memory, attention, curiosity, imitation, reason, etc. of which man boasts, may be found in an incipient, or sometimes even well-developed condition in," as they were often called in Darwin's day, "the lower animals."[6] He concluded that "there is no fundamental difference between man and the higher mammals in their mental faculties."[7]

Nevertheless, from the misconstrued concept that humans are evolutionarily better than animals it easily followed (to those who were predisposed to this position) that whites could be evolutionarily superior to blacks. In fact, based on the popularized (mis)interpretation of evolutionary theory came the trend of "Social Darwinism." Darwin had spoken of natural selection in relation to adaptation, but the Social Darwinists— usually the powerful or wealthy—adopted natural selection as the key to "progress." Darwin himself took great exception to this application of his theory, by which ruthless behavior towards different races, classes, or species could be rationalized and justified as being only a demonstration of evolution in action, a manifestation of "nature red in tooth and claw."

Before the concept of evolution was widely known and accepted, religious doctrine—which placed ("civilized," white, Christian) humans above all other beings—served as a justification for the subjugation of both blacks (whom pro-slavery writers and orators often claimed were of a different species!) and non-human animals; this subjugation was said to be ordained by God. Later, under the banner of Social Darwinism, both the unmitigated violence towards the "lower" animals and the enslavement of black "savages" in Africa were looked at as expressions of an evolutionary birthright.

Common only a quarter-century ago were charts depicting the evolution of primates from distant ancestors, up through various hominids, to a black person, and finally to a fully upright Aryan male. Without much of an uproar over their scientifi-cally-cloaked, subtly racist message (nor their poor science with regard to human evolution, human biology, and our relation to other modern primates), these charts were quietly retired. But they might give us some reason to pause as we consider a similar ranking system which places *all humans* up on the evolutionary pedestal, to the exclusion of other animals.

As we have seen, Darwin himself believed that evolution-ary history is no basis for deciding "who is better than whom." Evolution occurs as the result of genetic mutations and there is no moral basis for declaring that the mutated form is better than the unmutated ancestral form. But even comparison of a modern species to its own evolutionary predecessors makes better sense than what is usually attempted: comparison of humans to other animals from completely different biological families, in an effort to determine "which is best." Actually, in evolutionary time, humans are relatively new additions to the landscape; our current stage of development finds us without a harmonious or stable position within an ecosystem. Nor have we yet "worked out" all the quirks in our physiology or behavior, leaving our species with significant problems which simply don't exist for the members of most other highly complex species.

But is *any* of this relevant in determining if humans or any other animals are "worthy" of moral consideration? What are the qualities which a being need possess before treating them "like an animal" would be unacceptable? The more we learn about the earth's environment, its ecosystems, and the creatures who live here, the more we see the absurdity in the concept of ranking species against one another. All life on earth is inextricably bound together in a web of mutual interdependence. Within that web, each species of animal has a niche for which it is more or less adapted, and attributes which others lack. It is only an anthropocentric world view which makes qualities possessed by humans to be those by which all other species are measured.

If the earth was suddenly colonized by a species more powerful and bellicose than human beings, they could just as easily use attributes special to themselves when devising their ranking system. Let us suppose that by chance the aliens closely resembled a member of the cat family. They might decide to use the ability to see in near-darkness as the determining factor for who was worthy of freedom and who would be exterminated or enslaved. Measured against the standards of the alien cats, virtually all humans would be miserably lacking and, if those cats were anything like us when it came to ethics, humans would spend their lives in bondage. Their use of night-vision as a criterion would only be *as self-biased* as the criteria which we have decided to use. But it is we rather than the alien cousins of cats who are presently calling the shots, and as such we have made those characteristics which are claimed to be *exclusively human attributes* the requirements for moral consideration.

Many philosophers have clearly comprehended our bias. In the sixteenth century, Michel Eyquem de Montaigne wrote extensively on the subject. "I see some animals," Montaigne reflected, "that live so entire and perfect as life, some without sight, others without hearing: who knows whether to us also one, two, or three, or many other senses, may not be wanting."[8] Some two centuries later, Lichtenberg made it clear that he thought it foolish to unfavorably judge another creature by human standards. Equally foolish was it to believe that human attributes were any more or less remarkable than those special to another species. "The most accomplished monkey," observed Lichtenberg, "cannot draw a monkey, this too only man can do; just as it is also only man who regards his ability to do this as a distinct merit."[9] It is only human arrogance that is able to find beauty and perfection exclusively in those things human. "Just as foolish," continued Lichtenberg, "as it must look to a crab when it sees a man walk forward."[10]

Despite periodic voices of reason, action and tradition still demanded proof of our "superiority," in the form of vital differences, that would provide justification for man's dominion over the animals. What are those elusive solely-human qualities? Included among a veritable laundry list of attributes compiled in this exhaustive search for exclusivity are the ability to feel pain, to feel emotions, to reason, the possession of a soul, the ability to make free choices, and to speak a language—all claimed at one time or another to be features unique to human beings.[11]

In direct conflict with Darwin's views on the subject were those espoused, two centuries earlier, by René Descartes, a stalwart proponent of human superiority over non-human animals. Descartes believed animals lacked souls (while humans possessed them), intelligence, and even the ability to feel— pleasure, pain, or *anything*. If you struck one, the animal would cry out only in the same manner as a clock would chime, as a result of the workings of similar internal mechanisms. Bolstered by such Cartesian philosophy, physiological experiments on animals became an even more macabre endeavor, since any cries, any displays of suffering or efforts to escape, were viewed as the sounds and movements of veritable wind-up toys.

While very few people today would publically declare themselves in agreement with such extreme views, in our treatment of most non-human animals, we still behave like true Cartesians. And while most people, I believe, informally and *in theory* agree with Darwin's views which recognize that animals are thinking, feeling beings, we still search for the moral loophole—the quality or qualities possessed by humans and lacked by non-human animals—that will enable us to find a defensible reason to justify continuing to treat animals "like animals." Yet all false claims of behavioral uniqueness and exclusivity are easily dismissed with common sense and unprejudiced observation. On the subject of *reason*, one modern essayist argued:

> Although animals are unable to do algebra, they are able to make rational decisions regarding their own interests. Dogs, for example, would never be so irrational as to intentionally inhale smoke; they must be forced to do this by contemporary "researchers." I think it is safe to say that animals, in their own way, are at least as reasonable—that is, rational in pursuit of their own interests—as human beings.[12]

Attempts at moral disqualification on the basis of reason have not been used to exclude only non-human animals from the sphere of consideration. For centuries, black people were called "irrational," and this was used both as a reason to continue their "protective custody" (in the form of slavery), and to justify their virtually limitless abuse. Just as this claim has been popularly abandoned with regard to blacks, so too is it finally being widely disproved and retired with regard to animals.

Anyone who has spent time around animals knows that they both communicate with each other and try, with varying degrees of success, to communicate with our species. Montaigne suggested that both *they and we* fail equally at attempts to bridge the inter-species communication gap, and are equally frustrated. "This defect that hinders communication between them and us, why is it not just as much ours as theirs?" he asked. "We have some mediocre understanding of their meaning; so do they of ours, in about the same degree. They flatter us, threaten us, implore us, and we them."[13]

Not a hundred years later, Descartes, in his determined way, drew an altogether different conclusion. "All human beings," he began, "no matter how dull or stupid, even madmen, can arrange various words together and fashion them into a discourse... Contrariwise," he continued,

> no animal however perfect or well-bred can do anything of the sort. This is not simply because they lack the right organs, because magpies and parrots can learn to utter words as well as we can... and people born deaf and mute—who are at least as handicapped as the beasts are— have the custom of inventing their own signs, with which they communicate.[14]

"It seems incredible," concluded Descartes, "that the very best and brightest of monkeys or parrots could not learn to speak as well as the stupidest child... unless their souls were of an entirely different nature from our own."[15]

With the continued exception of some species of birds, animals still lack, of course, the vocal chords needed for verbal communication on our terms. Yet some of us are communicating with animals in ways which would make even Descartes take notice. Chimpanzees, orangutans, and gorillas have all been taught to communicate with humans through American Sign Language. Washoe, the first chimp to learn ASL, taught her adopted baby to sign. Perhaps best known is a gorilla named Koko, who since 1972 has been communicating with scientist Francine Patterson. Koko has a vocabulary in ASL of over 1000 words and understands spoken English, using ASL to respond. She can also read some printed words, including her own name, and creates new compound words to express thoughts and feelings her taught vocabulary did not provide for.

It's not only primates who are capable of such "human" communication. Jeffrey Moussaieff Masson cites the case of a parrot who unquestionably disproves the accepted belief that these birds can only repeat, devoid of context, remembered phrases. Left by his trainer at a veterinarian's office, the parrot pleaded, "Come here. I love you. I'm sorry. I want to go back."[16]

Yet even if some vast, undeniable distinction between humans and animals could finally be found, would that mean that we could then justify using, mistreating, even torturing, animals? Could we then say, as did eighteenth-century writer Thomas Love Peacock, that "nothing could be more obvious, than that all animals were created solely and exclusively for the use of man"?[17] From any perspective other than one predisposed to slave-holding, we could not; that special, mythical quality or attribute that was the sole domain of humans would *still* be irrelevant. For what does someone's ability to speak French, drive a car, see in the dark, do algebraic equations, or use a tool, have to do with whether or not it is acceptable or just to enslave, torture, or in some other way inflict cruelty upon them? The only *relevant* requirement which should be necessary to keep us from unnecessarily inflicting pain and suffering on someone is that individual's ability to feel pain and to suffer. Similarly, the only qualification individuals should need to make it wrong for us to dominate their lives is that they *possess life*, that they are alive. All of these other questions of abilities and attributes can fill philosophy books, but are, for these issues, irrelevant.

This is not intended to oversimplify matters and to imply that the oppressions experienced by blacks and animals have taken *identical* forms. A complex web of social, political, and economic factors sustained slavery and made possible the life of a slave as it was known. This book in no way attempts to make the case that these factors are the same for animals; there are distinct social, political, and economic factors which create and support the subjugation of animals, as well as differences between the possible manners in which blacks and animals could respond to their respective enslavements. But, as divergent as the cruelties and the supporting systems of oppression may be, there are commonalities between them. They share the same basic essence, they are built around the same basic relationship—that between oppressor and oppressed.

Branding a calf

"Sure, we used to throw 'em on the ground and cut their balls off with a pen-knife. Didn't give them any pain-killer, are you kidding? And that's not all; at the same time, we'd brand 'em and cut off their horns. And you know what? It didn't bother me . . . I never felt anything for them."

—An ex-ranch hand,
in a personal interview with the author

So, even though we may think of the experiences of black people in this country as being unique—as are, really, the experiences and reactions of every individual—there are many disturbing similarities between their treatment at the hands of white people in the United States and the treatment of animals at the hands of a large sector of the American population. Indeed, just as humans are oppressed the world over, animals receive poor treatment in nearly every human culture on earth.

Branding a captured woman

29

Further, any oppression helps to support other forms of domination. This is why it is vital to link oppressions in our minds, to look for the common, shared aspects, and work against them as one, rather than prioritizing victims' suffering—(what we have already identified as the "either-or" pitfall). For when we prioritize we are in effect becoming one with the "master." We are deciding that one individual or group is more important than another, deciding that one individual's pain is less important than that of the next. A common result of prioritization is infighting among the oppressed or defenders of the oppressed, doing tragically little to upset the very foundations of cruelty.

Comparing the suffering of animals to that of blacks (or any other oppressed group) is offensive only to the speciesist: one who has embraced the false notions of what animals are like. Those who are offended by comparison to a fellow sufferer have unquestioningly accepted the biased worldview presented by the masters. To deny our similarities to animals is to deny and undermine our own power. It is to continue actively struggling to prove to our masters, past or present, that we are *similar to those who have abused us*, rather than to our fellow victims, those whom our masters have also victimized.

Let us remember that to those with a master mentality, there is often very little difference between one victim and the next. When both blacks and animals are viewed as being "oppressible," the cruelties perpetrated upon them take similar forms. Later we will explore whether these similarities are due to mere chance or to something which operates deep in the minds of the masters. In the meantime, let us note that the domination of animals, which was being honed to a clumsy science centuries before black slavery in America began, was in many cases used as a prototype for the subjugation of blacks. So observed Keith Thomas in his important study *Man and the Natural World*:

Once perceived as beasts, people were liable to be treated accordingly. The ethic of human domination removed animals from the sphere of human concern. But it also legitimized the ill-treatment of humans who were in a supposedly animal condition. In the colonies, slavery, with its markets, its brandings and its constant labor, was one way of dealing with men thought to be beastly. The Portuguese, reported one English traveler, marked slaves "as we do sheep, with a hot iron," and at the slave market at Constantinople, Moryson saw the buyers taking their slaves indoors to inspect them naked, handling them "as we handle beasts, to know their fatness and strength."[18]

The suffering animals currently endure at the hands of human beings in laboratories, on "factory farms," as pets, and in the wild, sadly parallels that endured by black people in the antebellum United States and during the lingering postbellum period. The parallels of experience are numerous. Both humans and animals share the ability to suffer from restricted freedom of movement, from the loss of social freedom, and to experience pain at the loss of a loved one. Both groups suffer or suffered from their common capacity to be terrified by being hunted, tormented, or injured. Both have been "objectified," treated as property rather than as feeling, self-directed individuals. And both blacks, under the system of slavery, and animals were driven to a state of total psychic and physical defeat, as a result of all or some of the variables mentioned above. (With animals, of course, this continues today in its most extreme form.)

From all of this we see that the liberation of animals, while a pressing and worthy goal in its own right, is not of importance *only* to non-human animals. While people are no longer branded, inspected at auction, or displayed in zoos, subtler forms of oppression are still in operation which have their counter-parts in animals' slavery. Advances towards releasing animals from our domination and control of their lives will also serve to lessen the oppression of blacks and others who suffer under the weight of someone else's power. By eliminating the oppression of animals from the fabric of our culture, we begin to undermine some of the psychological structures inherent in a society which seems to create and foster masters. With a philosophy of universal respect for others' lives, treating anyone—human or non-human—in a cruel manner begins to be unthinkable.

The views presented in this book of such eminent thinkers, writers, and activists as Frederick Douglass, Harriet Beecher Stowe, Richard Wright, Paul Lawrence Dunbar, and many others, show us that they were acutely aware of the simi-larities between human and animal slavery. Let us follow their example and begin to reject oppression in all its forms.

> [Slaves] have been treated by the law upon the same footing as in England, for example, the . . . animals are still. The day may come when the rest of animal creation may acquire those rights which could never have been withholden from them but by the hand of tyranny. [Some] have already dis-covered that the blackness of skin is no reason why a human being should be abandoned without redress to the caprice of a tormentor. It may come one day to be recognized, that the number of legs, the villosity of the skin, or the termination of the *os sacrum*, are reasons equally insufficient for aban-doning a sensitive being to the same fate . . . The question is not, Can they *reason*? nor, Can they *talk*? but, Can they *suffer*?
>
> —Jeremy Bentham,
> *The Principles of Morals and Legislation*, 1789

# Oppression in Language and Literature

In dem days ole Brer Dog wuz e'en 'bout like he is dese days,
scratchin' fer fleas en growlin' over his vittles stidder sayin'
grace, en buryin' de bones w'en he had one too many. He
wuz des like he is now, 'ceppin' dat he wuz wile. He galloped
wid Brer Fox, en loped wid Brer Wolf, en cantered wid Brer
Loon. He went all de gaits, en he had des ez good a time ez
any un um en des ez bad a time.
— Joel Chandler Harris, "Why Mr. Dog is Tame,"
from *Nights with Uncle Remus: Myths and Legends
of the Old Plantation*, 1883

Lasting testimony to the severity of white oppression of blacks can be found in American literature. Not surpris-
ingly, this literature also preserves tangible evidence of the inter-
mingling, in the minds of some whites, of the two groups with
which we are here concerned: blacks and non-human animals.

Because society's opinion of animals was so low, racist
authors and anti-abolitionists propagandized against blacks by
comparing them to negative stereotypes of non-human animals.
Even today, we are still familiar with some of the negatively-
charged animal names black people have been called: *buck*, *fox*,
*monkey*, *ape*, and *coon*—imbued with none of the respect with
which Native Americans gave to the use of animal names.

33

"The Brute Negro" is one of seven stereotypes of black people found in American literature, as identified by Sterling Brown in his essay "Negro Character as Seen by White Authors." One of the most blatant ironies of these comparisons is that this stereotyping of blacks rests upon stereotypes of animals which are false in their own right. Reality was blindly ignored by these authors as they churned out banalities of savage apes and lewd, promiscuous beasts. As could be expected, the books made no mention of the very real and widespread practices of rape and brutalization of slaves by slave-owners. Some authors, such as H.R. Helper in his book *Nojuque* (1867), set up "black" and "beastly" as exact synonyms. In his book *The Negro A Beast* (1900), a racist theological tract, author Chas. Carrol declared, "All Scientific Investigation of the Subject Proves the Negro to Be An Ape." (This, of course, only echoed the sentiments of the racist contingency of scientists, such as Darwin's contemporary A.R. Wallace, who concluded that "natural selection could only have endowed the savage with a brain a little superior to that of an ape."[19])

Stereotypes of the 'brute Negro' in popular literature during the antebellum period are relatively rare because, explains Brown,

> the pro-slavery authors were anxious to prove that slavery had been a benefit to the Negro by removing him from savagery to Christianity...There were references to vicious criminal Negroes in fiction (vicious and criminal being synonymous to discontented and refractory), but these were considered as exceptional cases of half-wits led astray by abolitionists.
>
> Authors stressing the mutual affection between the races looked upon the Negro as a docile mastiff. [20]

With the Reconstruction, however, emancipation released (into literature and other forms of propaganda) the ferocity of the wild animal, and this mastiff turned into a "mad dog." "'Damyanks,' carpetbaggers, scalawags, and New England schoolmarms," notes Brown, "affected him with rabies."[21]

Thomas Dixon, another writer of what Brown terms "Ku Klux Klan fiction," is responsible for such works as *The Clansman* and *The Leopard's Spots*, in which are to be found such lurid chapter titles as "The Black Peril," "The Unspoken Terror," "A Thousand Legged Beast," and "The Hunt for the Animal." Brown's study demonstrates how Dixon's popular books helped to firmly fix the stereotype of the emancipated "black beast" in the minds of the masses:

> The stock Negro in Dixon's books, unless the shuffling hat-in-hand servitor, is a gorilla-like imbecile, who "springs like a tiger" and has the "black claws of a beast." In both books there is a terrible rape, and a glorious ride of the Knights on a Holy Crusade to avenge Southern civilization. Dixon enables his white geniuses to discover the identity of the rapist by using "a microscope of sufficient power (to) reveal on the retina of the dead eyes the image of this devil as if etched there by fire.". . . The doctor sees the "bestial figure of a negro—his huge black hand plainly defined. . . It was Gus." Will the wonders of science never cease? But perhaps, after all, Negroes have been convicted on even flimsier evidence.[22]

Through his analysis of contemporary popular literature, Brown observed the metamorphosis which occurred in people's minds in reaction to the transition of blacks from slaves to free individuals. When the person in question was still a slave—a

"good slave," mind you—he was portrayed, in Brown's words, as a "docile mastiff." When no longer enslaved, authors turned him into a "mad dog." Writing further, this time citing the work of Thomas Nelson Page, Brown comments that when "in their place, loyally serving and worshipping ole Marse," slaves were portrayed as "admirable creatures, but in freedom they are beasts."[23]

We don't even need to invent a metaphor to see how these attitudes relate to non-human animals; animals are *already used as the metaphor*. Brown's "mastiffs," "mad dogs," and "gorilla-like imbeciles" reveal not only the predilections of the authors whose work he critiques, but of Brown himself. Surely the sensitivity and intelligence of the gorilla Koko—one of the few gorillas who has come to be known as an individual person—dispels the long-held myth of the stupidity and violence of

these magnificent beings. Yet in seeing the comparisons of blacks to animals that were so prevalent in the period literature of his study, Brown accepted and, through his response, subsequently strengthened the negative views about animals held by the racist authors.

So "beastly" are animals considered, that to be like one implies the worst, that you are bad. It would logically follow that a person who is unlike an animal must by definition be good. First-century Christian philosopher Saint Augustine had already set the trend when he wrote "For so excellent is a man in comparison with a beast, that man's vice is beast's nature."[24] Brown's indignation at these offensive books blinded him to the fellow victims of their propaganda; in effect he responds by saying "We're nothing like those lowly beasts."

We've seen how these concepts affected humans; we need only to turn the metaphor on its head to see how animals are affected. When obedient and subservient, an animal is a loyal companion, a "good slave." When independent, an animal becomes suddenly transformed in our eyes into an uncontrollable beast. (Significantly, the words *black beast* translate into French as *bête* [animal] *noir* [black], a term meaning *nemesis*.) Think of the stories we were raised with, stories of "Big Bad Wolves" who prey on the innocent, silly, *domesticated* (and therefore good) piglets. Stories of "Lions and Tigers and Bears" who, in their wild and *uncontrolled* state, seem to live only to single-mindedly lunge at you from behind every tree.

Upon closer examination, we find the thoughts and language of oppression to be present not just in children's stories and other literature, but woven into the very fabric of our culture. For example, think of the term we use for the domestication of a wild horse: "to *break* a horse." This has quite a literal meaning, for when we tame a horse, we actually do *break* her. We break her spirit, bend her to our will, make her a subordinate and subservient servant. In the antebellum South, there were men called "nigger breakers," to whom "troublesome," "uppity" slaves were sent. Frederick Douglass was, in fact, sent to such a man.

Language, along with the written word, serves to perpetuate and reinforce prejudicial attitudes prevalent in our culture. And indeed, our language is deeply imbued with the terminology of the master's perspective. Yet we must take responsibility: ultimately, we create language, it does not create us. In the face of a culture rife with violence, even a wordless conviction about another way to interact with others still speaks eloquently.

# SLAVES AND MASTERS

There is no sin in using a thing for the purpose for which it is. Now the order of things is such that the imperfect are for the perfect... and [thus] all animals are for man.

—St. Thomas Aquinas,
*Summa Theologica II*, II, Q64, art.1, 1273

Man is born to subjection... The proclivity of the natural man is to domineer or to be subservient... If there are sordid, servile, and laborious offices to be performed, is it not better that there should be sordid, servile, and laborious beings to perform them?

—Chancellor Harper,
of the University of South Carolina, 1838

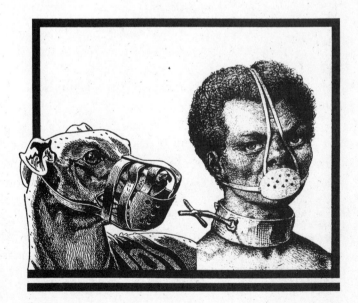

There are now between four and five millions of negroes in the United States. They or their descendants must remain forever—for good or evil—an element of our population. What are their natural relations to the whites?—what their normal condition?

The Almighty has obviously designed all his creatures—animal as well as human—for wise, beneficent, and useful purposes. In our ignorance of the animal world, we have only domesticated or applied to useful purposes a very small number, the horse, the ox, ass, dog, etc...The most ignorant farmer or laborer... knows the natures of these animals... and governs them accordingly.

[In the South] our people have practically solved their natural relations to the inferior race, and placed or rather retained the negro in his normal condition,... in domestic subordination and social adaptation, corresponding with [negroes'] wants, their instincts, their faculties, the nature with which God has endowed them.

—J.H. Van Evrie, M.D., *Negroes and Negro "Slavery": The First an Inferior Race, The Latter Its Normal Condition*, 1863

In his book *Cruelty*, Philip P. Hallie defines what to him is the essence of slavery:

People, not by virtue of their individual weaknesses or strengths, are put in the position of being as passive as groceries. When they are "good" they are good by the white master's standards for chattel, and their highest goals must be to satisfy his standards, the way a hard-working mule is a good mule... Utter passivity in total independence of individual traits, under the will of the white man—this was American slavery.[25]

Likewise, we might look at the relationship between a dog and his *master*, just one example of what is sometimes a modern slave/slave-owner relationship. The dog is considered by his *owner* to be a "good dog" if he walks to heel, displays no great interest when nearing other dogs, doesn't run except when allowed, doesn't bark except when required, and has no emotional needs except when desired by the master. Many dogs spend their entire lives in isolation, chained to a slab of concrete or a tree in their master's backyard. If a dog wishes to do something other than what pleases his master—play with other dogs (socialize), for instance—he may be beaten or otherwise punished. All independent actions are thus discouraged, and the dog learns that he will win approval—and avoid future beatings or other punishments—by suppressing his own desires and conforming to those of the omnipotent human who legally owns him. If at any point the master grows tired of his slave, he can simply be turned over to "the pound," which euphemistically

Slaves on a treadmill, and other punishments

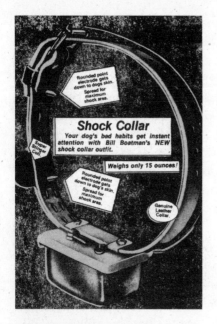

"A trained dog is a joy and pride. An untrained dog is an infernal nuisance to everybody. Most dogs are untrained."

—Stewart Brand,
*The Next Whole Earth Catalog*, 1981

"A state of bondage, so far from doing violence to the law of nature, develops and perfects it; and that, in that state [the Negro] enjoys the greatest amount of happiness, and arrives at the greatest degree of perfection, of which his nature is capable."

—R.R. Cobb,
*An Inquiry into the Law of Negro Slavery in the United States of America*, 1858

42

means that he will be quietly and secretly killed. Or if he is pure-bred, a high-quality slave, the master may sell him over to a new owner.

Another element of both human and animal slavery concerns the slave's inability to establish personal security or safety. In the slave/master relationship, there are no permanent rewards for fulfilling the master's expectations; rather than engendering gratitude, exceptional performance merely raises expectations. In his essay "Picking Cotton...", Solomon Northrup wrote of what this meant:

A slave never approaches the gin house with his basket of cotton but with fear. If it falls short in weight—if he has not performed the full task appointed him, he knows that he must suffer. And if he has exceeded it by ten or twenty pounds, in all probability his master will measure his next day's task accordingly.[26]

In order to see the similarities between this and what some animals face, let us look at the example of a "dairy cow", and examine just one facet of her life: milk production. A dairy cow is expected to produce a certain number of pounds of milk per day and, in the long-run, a certain tonnage per year. As she grows older, or perhaps suffers from an illness, she becomes less productive, ceasing to make as large a profit for her owner as she once did. Eventually, despite her years of service, when her milk output drops below a certain point of profitability she is sold and slaughtered. If at some point during her life she outdoes herself by producing more than the expected amount of milk, this is the standard by which she will thereafter be judged; more likely than not, her high productivity will result in her being used in intensive super-ovulation breeding programs as well.

43

It is clear from these few examples that the slavery-related sufferings of black people are often paralleled by the sufferings of animals lost in the machinery of modern institutionalized cruelty. Innumerable other parallels exist, from the disruption of self-regulated reproduction; to birth and the consequential destruction of the familial structure; throughout life and the many cruelties, such as vivisection and hunting, to which individuals are subjected.

By viewing the experiences of animals—such as dogs and "milk cows"—through the lens of human slavery, we come to realize that master/slave relationships permeate our culture. Cultural blinders hinder our ability to see society's (current) slaves as the individuals they are, while simultaneously obscuring our own motivations from us. Whether it is a white master brutally punishing his slave for using a tone of voice he doesn't like, or a dairy farmer slaughtering his cows, the ramifications are immense. Weaving these disparate relationships together is a common thread: only the master's perspective is considered.

> [The horse] is by Nature a very lazy animal whose idea of heaven is an enormous field of lush grass in which he can graze undisturbed until his belly is full, and after a pleasant doze can start filling himself up all over again.
>
> —Captain Elwin Hartley Edwards,
> *From Paddock to Saddle*, 1972

> The Negro if left to himself will not work, he will lie down and bask in the sun... It is very evident that [if slavery were abolished]... the free white operative would be compelled to pay all the expenses necessary to support this idle, drunken, lazy population.
>
> —John Campbell, *Negromania*, 1851

# SOCIAL RELATIONS: THE DESTRUCTION OF SECURITY

The first instinct the farmer frustrates in all animals... is that of the newborn animal turning to its mother for protection and comfort and, in some cases, for food. The chick comes out of the incubator and never sees a hen; the calf which is to be fattened for veal or beef is taken from the cow at birth, or very soon after; and even the piglet is weaned far earlier now than it used to be. The factors controlling this are mainly economic.

—Ruth Harrison, *Animal Machines*, 1964

I never saw my mother, to know her as such, more than four or five times in my life; and each of these times was very short in duration, and at night. She was hired by a Mr. Stewart who lived about 12 miles from my home. She made her journeys to see me in the night, traveling the whole distance on foot, after the performance of her day's work. She was a field hand, and a whipping is the penalty of not being in the field at sunrise... I do not recollect of ever seeing my mother in the light of day.

—Frederick Douglass, *An American Slave*, 1845

O ne of the most tragic aspects of life as a slave comes about through destruction of the family, and in a larger sense, the social structure. In the time of the African slave trade, it was common to kidnap children while their parents were off gathering food or tending to some other chore.[27] Once kidnapped, the children would be sold "down the coast;" if they survived the ordeal which followed, they would eventually end up on a Southern plantation. Thus, relationships with their entire families—extended and immediate—were at once ended; the family was never reunited.

In the States, families formed under the institution of slavery were subject to different destructive practices. "Little children," writes one historian, "were torn from their mothers' arms soon after they were weaned, to be kept. . . as 'a pet'" by privileged Southern women.[28] Slaves were brought to auction: children sold away from their mothers, husbands away from their wives, lovers auctioned off separately. A witness to a slave auction in 1853 recorded the following conversation with a 25-year-old female slave with three children who was to be sold that day:

"It was often remarked that the affection of the slaves was stronger toward the whites than toward their own offspring."

—Thomas Nelson Page,
*The Negro: The Southerner's Problem*, 1904

If a slave gave birth to her child at the same time as the mistress of the plantation, she had to nurse the white child rather than her own.

One of the traders asked her what was the matter with her eyes? Wiping away the tears, she replied, "I s'pose I have been crying." "Why do you cry?" "Because I have left my man behind, and his master won't let him come along." "Oh, if I buy you, I will furnish you with a better husband, or man, as you call him, than your old one." "I don't want any *better* and I won't have any *other* as long as he lives." "Oh, but you will though, if I buy you."[29]

It can only be guessed at whether these practices were employed to give blacks a sense of total defeat and hopelessness in an effort to forestall rebellion, or if they were perpetrated upon blacks "merely" through obtuse callousness on the part of slave-owners. It would seem that in most cases the latter explanation held true, because of then-common perceptions. In the eyes of the white slave-holders, black people were "just animals,"

"Veal" calves, separated from their mothers after birth, chained to their stalls. Their mothers' milk is consumed by humans.

47

who could soon get over separation from a child or other loved one. In fact, when dealing with the subject of intimate relationships between blacks, antebellum racist thinkers denied that love existed. They maintained that it was just "animal lust" and "animal attraction" which were responsible for intimate bonding between two slaves, two more examples of metaphors based in societal speciesism.

Similarly, most people today find it hard to accept the notion that non-human animals feel love for one another as individuals. Even life-long pairing is dismissed as "instinct." Anyone who has heard the protracted, pained protestations of a cow and her calf who have been separated might have had to give it a second thought, but it seems we assume that as soon as the outward signs of suffering have died down, so too have the inner torment and pain. But, as anyone who has sustained the death of a loved one or a particularly painful separation from someone knows, the pain can continue long after we have stopped crying or complaining. And if it is true that the pain lingers in so *verbal* an animal as a human being, for whom vocalization of anguish is "standard" behavior, what are we to surmise when hypothesizing about a much *less* verbal animal such as a cow, for whom vocalization of anguish is naturally a much rarer event, and by whom pain is usually suffered in silence?

Every day, in countless ways, humans destroy the relationships of other animals. In the wild, sport hunters randomly shoot the mates of waterfowl, some of whom pair for life. Often, the surviving mate dies of starvation while mourning. In the annual Canadian harp seal slaughter, hunters have been filmed wielding screaming baby seals like clubs to attack the pups' own mothers, before smashing the young pups to death on the ice. Using methods which often mirror those used in the human slave trade, we violently destroy primate communities in order to capture the infants for display in zoos, use in laboratories, or lives of captivity as pets. The strategy is to kill the mothers and other protective adults, leaving the infants defenseless, and at least ten chimps die for every infant that survives more than a year at its final destination overseas.[30] This is not an activity new to the twentieth century; nineteenth-century philosopher and educator Professor J. Howard Moore wrote with empathy about the frantic anguish of a mother monkey as she tried unsuccessfully to defend her wounded and dying baby from the man who would soon kill her as well. Moore concluded that most "human beings . . . are inclined to pass over lightly all displays of feeling" by these fellow primates.[31]

In breeding facilities for laboratories, we "produce" *millions* of rodents—mice, rats and rabbits—each year, delivered by caesarean section into individual cages, to provide scientists with "sterile" animals who have never been allowed contact with another of their kind. There is even an entire area of psychological experimentation—"maternal deprivation"—in which researchers create and observe in animals extreme cases of mother-child separation and pathology. Although many different species of animals have been used in these studies, non-human primates are the favorite victim of researchers' curiosity. From the published results of one such experiment comes the following:

> Separation of mother and infant monkeys is an extremely stressful event for both mother and infant, as well as . . . for all other monkeys [nearby]. The mother becomes ferocious toward attendants and extremely protective of her infant. The infant's screams can be heard almost over the entire building. The mother struggles and attacks the separators. The baby clings tightly to the mother and to any object to

which it can grasp to avoid being held or removed by the attendant. With the baby gone, the mother paces the cage almost constantly, charges the cage occasionally, bites at it, and makes continual attempts to escape... The infant emits... shrill screams intermittently and almost continuously for the period of separation.[32]

In food production the tragedy continues. Chicks never see a hen; pigs have but a brief interlude with their mother sow, who is kept tethered to a metal stall to ensure minimal calorie-burning and food consumption. Dairy cows are artificially inseminated (and thus deprived of any contact with a bull) to produce a long succession of calves needed to stimulate milk production, only to have each calf ripped away from her immediately following birth. If the calf is a male—and is not needed for veal production—he will be immediately killed. If female, the calf may have the same fate as her mother: life in a milk factory, doomed to churn out babies she will never nuzzle, never run with in a field.

> Lawdy, lawdy, them was tribbollashuns! Wunner dese here womans was my Antie en she say dat she skacely call to min he e'r whoppin' her, 'case she was er breeder woman en' brought in chillun ev'y twelve mont's jes lak a cow bringin' in a calf...
>
> —Martha Jackson, (born 1850), in *Alabama Narratives*

> Do you think nothing of their families left behind? Of the connections broken? Of the friendships, attachments, and relationships that are burst asunder?
>
> —William Pitt, Speech on the Slave Trade, House of Commons, 2 April 1792

# TRANSPORTATION, OR THE UNBEARABLE JOURNEY

Deponent further sayeth *The Bella J*
left the Guinea Coast
with a cargo of five hundred blacks and odd
for the barracoons of Florida:

"That there was hardly room 'tween-decks for half
the sweltering cattle stowed spoon-fashion there;
that some went mad of thirst and tore their flesh
and sucked the blood..."

—Robert Hayden,
from his poem *Middle Passage*

Sheep boarding ship for voyage from Australia to Middle East

Animals that die in transit do not die easy deaths. They freeze to death in winter and collapse from thirst and heat exhaustion in summer. They die, lying unattended in stockyards, from injuries sustained in falling off a slippery loading ramp. They suffocate when other animals pile on top of them in an overcrowded, badly loaded truck. They die from thirst or starve when careless stockmen forget to give them water or food. And they die from the sheer stress of the whole terrifying experience, for which nothing in their life has given them the slightest preparation.

—Peter Singer, 1974

It is known that... where they carry the prisoners to the ships, those on land weep copiously, horrified and fearful of the violence that is done to them, seeing that in addition to taking men against their will, they treat them very inhumanely on the ships, whence a great number die suffocated by their own stench and from other bad treatment. There was one night in which thirty died on one ship in port because they would not open the hatch for fear [the slaves] would escape, no matter how loudly those below shouted for them to open because they were dying; the only response they received was to be called dogs and similar names.

—A Portuguese Clergyman
of the Eighteenth Century.[33]

Only about fifteen million of some thirty or forty million black Africans survived the ordeal of capture and transport to become slaves in the Western Hemisphere. Those who survived had managed to live through the hellish "Middle Passage," transport by cargo boat to the New World. When demand for slaves soared in the eighteenth century, those ship captains who "tight-packed" their human cargo won out over the "loose-

Floor plan of a ship's slave-hold

"Silo"-type egg factory, New Mexico

packers." Many historical accounts indicate that two and some-times three tiers of slave holding-areas were built in a six-foot hold. Reverend John Newton, author of the hymn beginning "How sweet the name of Jesus sounds," instead described the area below deck as being sometimes five-feet or less in height, and "divided towards the middle, for the slaves lie in two rows, one above the other, close to each other like books upon a shelf."[34] Newton's account is certainly first-hand; before going on to become a pioneer in the movement to abolish the slave trade, he was a mate and then a master of a slave ship. Slaves were frequently so tightly packed, even on the journeys of this com-paratively pious master—who forbade swearing among his crew and read the liturgy with them every Sunday—that, in Newton's own words, "the shelf would not easily contain one more."[35]

The slave-holds, sometimes called "kennels,"[36] were con-structed of unplaned boards, and the newly-captured slaves were provided with no bedding for their journey; in a stormy passage,

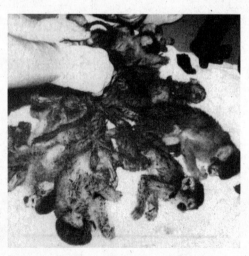

These monkeys—destined for vivisection—died in transit.

"the skin over their elbows might be worn down to the bare bones."[37] The above conditions, coupled with poor ventilation and a total absence of sanitation, made death from septic wounds and epidemics the norm.

Today, it is common to call such a ship a "cattle boat," just as Jews and others were transported to the concentration camps in what have frequently been referred to as "cattle cars." Once again, this is not just an eccentricity of our language. One historian, in fact, writing about the Middle Passage, saw fit to comment that "the slaves were treated like cattle."[38] Cattle, and other animals, are indeed transported in vehicles such as these, in no greater comfort than their historical human counterparts.

Steers are shipped, without regard to summer heat or winter cold, distances as great as 2,000 miles. Sometimes they experience such a journey several times in their short lives, shipped from auction, to feedlot, to auction, and finally to the slaughterhouse—their final destination. The stress of transport

Many slaves spent the entire voyage from Africa to America in positions similar to this.

Pregnant sows

"The poor creatures, thus cramped, are likewise in irons for the most part which makes it difficult for them to turn or attempt to rise or lie down without hurting themselves or each other. Every morning, perhaps, more instances than one are found of the living and the dead fastened together."

—Rev. John Newton,
*Thoughts upon the African Slave Trade*, 1788

is great, resulting in tremendous losses in body weight—up to nine percent of total body weight in a one- or two-day trip; the animals actually lose weight from their bones. Stressed cattle also frequently fall victim to what is known as "shipping fever," of which hundreds of thousands die yearly.

Many survivors of the human slave trade's "tight-packing" also came through the ordeal weakened and emaciated. They were "fattened up in a . . . slave-yard,"—the historical counterpart to the modern cattle feedlot—"before being offered for sale."[38]

Parallels between the human and animal slave trades can also be seen in international wild animal trafficking, a multi-billion-dollar business. The wild animal trade caters to those seeking exotics for pets, private hunting parks, display in zoos, and use in medical and psychological experimentation. Animals are frequently smuggled across borders—bound and gagged—hidden in luggage, inside tires or upholstery, or in the cargo holds of airplanes and ships. Mortality is high, but the profit on the sale of the survivors is as well.

It is not only in our day that the similarities between the trade in humans and animals have been recognized. However, we might take heart that the conclusions drawn from such recognition are, in our own time, becoming more enlightened than those in the not-so-distant past. In one incident on record from the period of legal trade in human beings, the owners of a shipment of slaves sought to collect insurance for slaves thrown overboard in the course of the overseas passage. "The jury found for the owners, since," noted an historian upon examination of the records, "they had no doubt. . . that the case of slaves was the same as if horses had been thrown overboard."[40]

Other domestic animals are subjected to even more intensive conditions during their lives than are "beef" cows. The horrors of the Middle Passage, with its cramped conditions, pools of excrement and urine, "acceptable" mortality-rates, seemingly interminable length of duration, and finally insanity leading to violence and cannibalism, have been projected into modernity in the form of factory farming. Sows are chained or clamped into narrow farrowing stalls for months and years on end, to conserve space and food-calorie energy expenditure. Chickens, and increasingly pigs, are stacked 3, 4, or 5 tiers high in rows of tiny "battery" cages. Pigs' tails are "docked"—cut off without anesthesia—to prevent stress-induced tail-biting.

Australia, the world's largest producer of wool, annually ships seven million sheep to the Middle East on tightly packed "slave ships," with 50,000 or more sheep on each three-week boat trip. Aside from the "usual" deaths which occur on these journeys, there are periodic disasters (disease, fire, ventilation-system breakdown) which result in the deaths of thousands. Upon reaching their destination, those who survived are killed in the Moslem "Halal" ritualistic slaughter style, typically a more protracted and painful process than most commercial slaughter, or even Kosher slaughter, which has itself become known for its unnecessary cruelty.[41]

In the United States (as in much of the world), animals on the way to the slaughterhouse are usually not fed as this would "waste" food, the cost of which those in the industry would rather keep as profit. Depending on the distance between the farm or feedlot and the slaughterhouse which will pay the most, animals may travel 12, 36, or even 72 hours.[42]

When those blacks who did survive Middle Passage reached the shore, what awaited them was the terror of the slave market or auction, and a life of slavery. When animals reach the end of their journey, what awaits them is either imprisonment or isolation in human society, torture, or the ultimate extreme to which slavery can be taken: the deprivation of life itself—slaughter.

> The deck, that is, the floor of their rooms [in the slave ship], was so covered with the blood and mucus which had proceeded from them in consequence of the flux, that it resembled a slaughterhouse.
>
> —Dr. Alexander Falconbridge,
> *An Account of the Slave Trade on the Coast of Africa*, 1788

# HUNTING

Two men on a drunken hunting trip failed to find any deer and instead cold-bloodedly murdered a deaf black man, yesterday as he walked along a railroad track in Chico.

—*Los Angeles Times*[43]

Hunting. A seemingly straightforward word, but one which connotes many often contradictory images. A carefree day in the woods with "the boys"? A show of skill? A demonstration of absolute power over someone else: the ability to *end* someone's life. Many people are uncomfortable with the pronoun *someone* being used to refer to a non-human animal. Perhaps they feel more comfortable with the term some*thing*. But a thing doesn't *have* a life. If you shoot it, it doesn't die because it was never alive. It can't bleed, it can't feel pain. Perhaps it was once alive, but now dead it is a thing. A corpse is a thing. So hunting can be looked at as turning some*one* into some*thing*. Turning a vital, living being with a past and a potential future into a corpse. It takes the independent relatively autonomous (uncontrolled) being and turns her or him into an *object*, some*thing* which is no longer capable of any independent thought or action. And in this way the hunter has proven himself. He has proven that he has the power, the ultimate power of life and death, and can exert it over someone else.

In the following passage from the book *Black Like Me*, the author, John Howard Griffin, relates an experience he had which amply illustrates that what is of essence here is not the *species* of prey, but the issue of power. The outcome of who will be the next victim of this hunter's ego is always in question, as the potential victim changes hazily from black person to deer and back again. Perhaps the only thing which saved Griffin from his death was that power over a human being (who speaks the same language) can be effectively asserted through verbal means.

I hitchhiked up toward the swamp country between Mobile and Montgomery. . . . I walked some miles before a large, pleasant-faced man halted his truck and told me to get in. When I opened the door I saw a shotgun propped against the seat next to his knee. I recalled it was considered sport among some elements in Alabama to hunt "nigs" and I backed away.

"Come on," he laughed. "That's for hunting deer."

[As the conversation continued, it soon deteriorated, and the driver revealed his racist attitudes.]

". . . What're you doing down here?"

"Just traveling around, trying to find jobs."

"You're not down here to stir up trouble, are you?"

"Ohgodno."

"You start stirring up these niggers and we sure as hell know how to take care of you."

"I don't intend to."

"Do you know what we do to trouble makers down here?"

"No sir."

"We either ship them off to the pen or kill them."

He spoke in a tone that sickened me, casual, merciless. . . The immensity of it terrified me. But it caught him up like lust now. He entertained it, his voice unctuous with pleasure and cruelty. The highway stretched deserted through the swamp forests. He nodded toward the solid wall of brush flying past our windows.

"You can kill a nigger and toss him into that swamp and no one'll ever know what happened to him."[44]

Each year in the United States, at least 200 million animals are killed under the guise of "sport." Twice as many are not killed outright but are wounded and eventually die of gangrene, infection, blood-loss, or starvation. The U.S. Fish & Wildlife Service reports that prior to the 1991 ban on the use of lead bullets for hunting waterfowl, 2- to 3-million birds died of lead poisoning each year from the ingestion of lead bullets in streams and marshes, deposited there by hunters who missed their "target."[45] While the tons of lead shot deposited in the nation's waterways prior to the ban remain, these deaths, in addition to the millions of birds who are directly killed by hunters, will continue.[46]

The most commonly hunted species of animal in the United States is deer, the target of some 81% of all hunters.[47] The *type* of deer most hunters go after—the male deer, the stag, the buck—supports the idea of hunting as a display of power. Hunters try to kill the most "virile" of the males, those with the biggest antlers. If they are successful at ending this life, they have proven their own manhood.

Is it just chance which gave us the racist slang term for a black man?—*buck*; or, for that matter, the term by which blacks of both genders were referred—*coon*. A modern lexicographer writes, under the heading "Raccoon," that "in the South hunting coons on moonlit nights has long been a favorite sport, their meat being roasted and eaten." She then notes that "coon" became a disparaging word for black people in the nineteenth century, even inspiring a song by Ernest Hogan: "All Coons Look Alike to Me."[48] Runaway slaves were in fact hunted down in much the same manner as were raccoons, and as animals continue to be today. Until 1831 throughout the South, notes one historian, "there were men who made it a profession to keep 'nigger dogs' [who were specially trained to hate negroes] and with them to follow up and catch runaway slaves."[49]

It is not surprising that in the highly stylized hunts of the British upper classes, which have remained virtually unchanged for centuries, one finds close parallels to the hunting of slaves in the Southern United States. On horseback, and with a team of trained dogs, British huntsmen track weasels, otters, deer, foxes, hares, minks, and other animals. Dens are destroyed; infants killed alongside parents; animals "coursed" over great distances, until exhaustion or injury delivers them into the jaws of the dogs (who are often mistreated themselves). Or, perhaps even more unfortunately, the wounded and exhausted prey falls into the hands of hunt participants, who are sometimes known to flay or dismember still-living animals. After the kill in British blood-sports, the "trophies" extracted from the victim—teeth, the heart, or feet, for example—are distributed among the hunters.

In the United States, the object of most hunters' desires is a buck's head, complete with antlers, to stuff and hang over the sofa. Wealthy trophy hunters, however, travel the world over to bring back more exotic heads, skins, and other trophies. Just a few decades ago, gorillas were routinely slaughtered only to provide collectors with paper-weights made of their hands and feet. And today, hunters may pay up to $50,000 to legally kill an endangered polar bear in Canada, purchasing a hunting license from a Native American tribe that peddles them for cash.[50]

Essayist Michelle Russell demonstrates our deeply ingrained cultural acceptance of the hunting of animals as sport, even while illustrating the parallels between the traditions of recreational hunting and racist action. She reminds us of:

the biological metaphors which told us, in no uncertain terms, what kind of animal Anglo-Americans thought us to be. The consequences of those ideas in action: the spits and crossties where we were roasted after the hunt. Our mutilated body parts smoked and sold as trophies.[51]

Hunting has not been without its share of serious critics. Perhaps the most concise and chilling critique was made by Joseph Wood Krutch in his book *The Great Chain of Life*. "Killing for 'sport'," he wrote, "is the perfect type of that pure evil for which metaphysicians have sometimes sought." He continued:

Most wicked deeds are done because the doer proposes some good to himself. . . The killer for sport has no such comprehensible motive. He prefers death to life, darkness to light. He gets nothing except the satisfaction of saying "Something which wanted to live is dead. There is that much less vitality, consciousness, and, perhaps, joy in the universe. I am the Spirit that Denies."[52]

Today, recreational hunting is participated in by a relatively small percentage of the population; most people don't hunt and don't want to. Yet laws are geared to accommodate the minority. How have the interests of so few come to overshadow the beliefs of the majority? The answer lies with each state's Fish, Game, and Wildlife Service, in whose hands the fate of the nation's animals is primarily held. Staffed and administered largely by pro-hunting "sportsmen," these agencies operate with the underlying premise that the nation's wildlife exists for the pleasure of the sportsman minority.

Notably, traditional, culturally-intact Native Americans and many other aboriginal peoples hunted out of real necessity, with respect for, and in harmony with, the balance of nature. Theirs was not a profane act, nor an unconscious attempt to symbolically conquer chaos. Hunting as an exercise of power is a completely different act, one which only serves to further and further upset the balance of nature, the balance of humans *to* nature, and ultimately, the balance of humans themselves. It is not sufficient to pay lip-service to the concept of respect and harmony prior to (let me here run the risk of exaggeration) switching off the television set, grabbing a beer, and driving to the woods to blow away a deer. Harmony and respect were central to an entire world-view, a view of the universe, with which the very lives of Native Americans were imbued, from birth until death, and, in their philosophy, from death until rebirth.

The act of hunting, as performed in the manner explored in this chapter, was, and continues to be, an expression of the power which the ruling race or species exerts over the powerless. Prior to 1863 it was recognized that hunting down black people— "slaves"—was a sanctioned act. Perhaps our society will soon realize, with due horror, that we have been late in extending our respect and consideration to *all* of those who need protection.

# VIVISECTION

They administered beatings to dogs with perfect indifference, and made fun of those who pitied the creatures as if
they felt pain. They said the animals were clocks; that the
cries they emitted when struck, were only the noise of a little
string that had been touched, but that the whole body was
without feeling. They nailed poor animals up on boards by
their four paws to vivisect them and see the circulation of
the blood which was a great subject of controversy.
—Nicholas Fontaine,
*Memoires pour servir a l'histoire de Port-Royal,* 1738

Negroes...are void of sensibility to a surprising degree.
They are not subject to nervous diseases. They sleep sound
in every disease, nor does any mental disturbance ever
keep them awake. They bear chirurgical operations much
better than white people, and what would be the cause of
unsupportable pain to a white man, a Negro would almost
disregard.
—Dr. Mosely, *Treatise on Tropical Diseases,* 1787

The term "vivisection" means "live dissection,"
but has come to be used to define any experiment performed on
a living creature, human or non-human. This includes burning,
freezing, non-therapeutic operations, studies which involve
inducing disease or intentional injuries in a healthy individual,
psychology experiments, drug testing, and virtually any other
procedure which involves tinkering with someone's life in a
non-therapeutic manner.

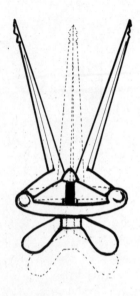

*Speculum oris*, used to pry open
the mouths of suicidal slaves

Currently, each year in the United States alone, at least 30 million non-human animals die at the hands of scientists and laboratory technicians, and in breeding facilities which service our nations laboratories.[53] That's about one animal every second of every day. In Great Britain an animal dies in a lab once every ten seconds.[54]

Animals are used extensively in commercial product testing. They have been strapped into simulated car-crash devices, impacted repeatedly to test brain damage at different velocities. They have new hair sprays, oven cleaners, shampoos, and other consumer and industrial products fed to them, sprayed into their eyes, and injected under their skin, to test for levels of toxicity. While not required by law, these latter tests are routinely conducted—primarily to reduce legal liability in the case of poisoning—when synthetic or otherwise potentially-dangerous materials are used in manufacturing. (Many firms have again

66

Stereotaxic device
immobilizes animal,
and permits, among a
gamut of experiments,
the force-feeding of
any substance
through a tube

begun manufacturing products from natural, nontoxic ingredients, and do not test their products on animals.)

Experiments performed under the auspices of medical research can include anything from studies in "learned helplessness," to experimental surgery, to the observation of the results of "noxious stimuli" on unanesthetized animals, burn studies in which "test-subjects" are created by blowtorching live animals, to the inducement of diseases and the testing of new drugs for drug and chemical companies.

Of the above, learned helplessness experiments are perhaps the least known to the public. In this area of psychological research, animals are punished, inescapably and usually with electric shocks, for normal behavior such as trying to eat food after they have been starved, or for trying to escape from another source of pain. Eventually, researchers find that with enough random and inescapable punishment, animals can be made to

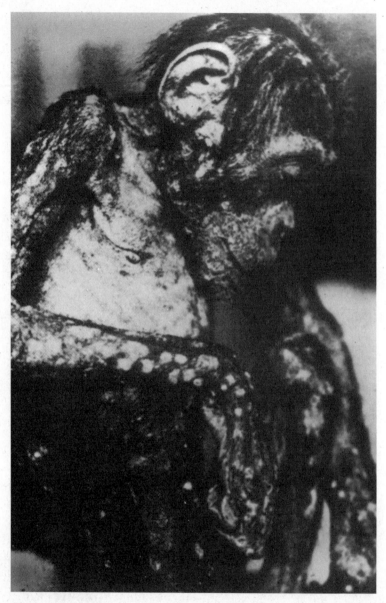

Chimpanzee infected with syphilis in experiment

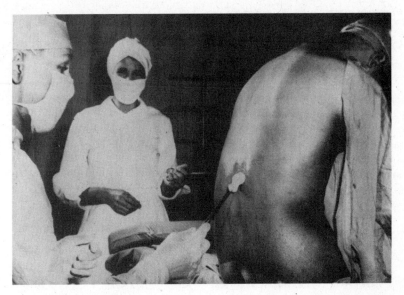

Tuskegee Syphilis Study:
*above*: An unidentified subject receives a spinal tap.
*below left*: Case of ulcerated cutaneous syphilis on leg,
photographed from rear.
*below right*: Case of ulcerated cutaneous syphilis on right arm.

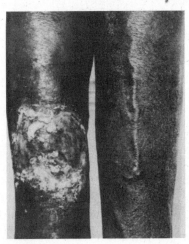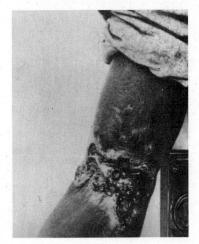

stop trying to get away from the source of their torment, even after the barriers which originally prevented their escape have been removed.

Without any mandatory or established system for sharing protocols or experiment results, there is a vast duplication of research; similar—even identical—studies are performed at facilities throughout the nation and the world. Relatively few studies are significant enough (even within the researchers' own fields of study) to ever reach publication in a medical journal, much less achieve any degree of relevant application.

At a rally in San Francisco protesting the use of animals in research, Alameda County supervisor John George said, "My people were the first laboratory animals in America." Indeed, blacks suffered at the hands of scientists just as animals continue to do today. Perhaps the best documented and widely known example of medical experimentation on black people is the Tuskegee Syphilis Study.[55] It was, in fact, the longest involuntary experiment performed on human beings in medical history.

Funded by the U.S. Public Health Service, the study was conducted in Macon County, Alabama, beginning in 1932. This was a very poor, rural area where living conditions for the black cotton-field workers were not too different from when slavery was still legal. The white scientists, working with the racist hypothesis that syphilis affected whites and blacks differently, observed the course of untreated syphilis in the black male for forty years, until the experiment was exposed by a journalist and finally ended and investigated. The men were never told they had syphilis, were not offered any treatment, nor were they told how the disease was transmitted.

Richard Wright, renowned author of *Native Son*, worked as a menial laborer in what he would only identify as "one of the largest and wealthiest hospitals in Chicago." In this excerpt from his essay "The Man Who Went to Chicago" he gives us a glimpse into his reaction to his experiences there:

> Each Saturday morning I assisted a... doctor in slitting the vocal cords of a fresh batch of dogs from the city pound. The object was to devocalize the dogs so that their howls would not disturb the patients in other parts of the hospital. I held each dog as the doctor injected Nembutal into its veins to make it unconscious: then I held the dog's jaws open as the doctor inserted the scalpel and severed the vocal cords. Later, when the dogs came to, they would lift their heads to the ceiling and gape in a soundless wail. The sight became lodged in my imagination as a symbol of silent suffering.[56]

In light of current knowledge about health and the causes of disease, utilizing animals in research, even for medical research focussing on life-threatening human illnesses, now appears an archaic holdover from a less sophisticated era, fairly calling back to the days of dungeons and sweat-boxes. The Western medical paradigm of seeing diseases as foreign invaders within our bodies lacks the vision and sophistication of ancient Oriental medicine, and other non-allopathic healing systems, which see chronic imbalances within us as the source of the illnesses which Western medicine can only detect in their most acute forms, usually with no clue as to what engendered them.[57]

The Western approach is akin to those in the Middle Ages who believed in "spontaneous generation." Because people didn't understand the simple apparatus by which maggots spontaneously "appeared" on rotting meat, a plausible and widely-accepted scientific theory was that life could spontaneously spring forth, apparently from "the hand of God," since there was no other tangible source or explanation. Spontaneous generation was thus accepted, along with the fertilization of an egg with sperm, as one of the several ways in which new life was generated. (It was not until someone thought to observe meat as it rotted *beneath a bell-jar* that this theory began to be dispelled.) In the same way, the Western medical system lacks the understanding both of how diseases develop and how health can be restored. We are each born a unique individual with hereditary strengths and weaknesses, and can be further weakened by diet, drugs, or exposure to chemicals. Every systemic weakness is a potential foothold for pathogens, and a gateway for degenerative disease. Oriental medicine works with nature to restore bodily and mental integrity and harmony, whereas Western medicine operates as though diseases "spontaneously appear" in our bodies, and then sets to trying to attack and kill those diseases.

While *billions* of tax-dollars are spent each year to literally torture animals—supposedly for our benefit—many *humans* in this country lack access to even basic health care and nutrition. Further, due to our priorities (and those of the drug companies which fund much research), people lack access even to information which might save their lives, such as the fact that many of our nation's biggest killers—heart disease, high blood pressure, cancer, and diabetes—can all be prevented or corrected through diet. The tragedy is that our entire approach to medicine, which unfortunately brings with it the grim realities of vivisection, gives people the message that they must wait for doctors to find a miracle cure, instead of empowering people to make positive changes in their diets, and to fully utilize alternative therapies such as nutrition, herbology, homeopathy, and acupuncture.[58]

> He that breaks a thing to find out what it is has left the path of wisdom.
>
> —J.R.R. Tolkein, (1892-1973)

# IN DEFENSE OF SLAVERY

[The abolition of the slave trade] would be extreme cruelty to the African savages, a portion of whom it saves from massacre, or intolerable bondage in their own country, and introduces into a much happier state of life.

—James Boswell, (1740-1795)

In the eighteenth century it was widely urged that domestication was *good* for animals; it civilized them and increased their numbers: "we multiply life, sensation and enjoyment."

—Keith Thomas, *Man and the Natural World*,
quoting Benjamin Rush, M.D., (1746-1813)

[It was] best for the beasts that they should be under man.

—*The Theological, Philosophical, Miscellaneous Works of the Reverend William Jones*, 1801

It has long been contended that, for some—and of course, never *us*, but always *them*—life as a slave proves more beneficial than detrimental. In fact, two thousand years before any of the above sentiments were expressed, Aristotle had used this same approach in his attempt to justify the subjugation and domestication of animals *and* some humans. For this rationalization to be effective, the victims need to be transformed—in the mind of the captor/master—from oppressed beings to thankful underlings; grateful for being used, appreciated, and protected, while fulfilling the needs of their superiors. Wrote Aristotle:

73

For all tame animals there is an advantage in being under human control, as this secures their survival. And as regards the relationship between male and female, the former is naturally superior, the latter inferior, the former rules and the latter is subject.

By analogy, the same must necessarily apply to mankind as a whole. Therefore all men who differ from one another by as much as the soul differs from the body or man from a wild beast (and that is the state of those who can work by using their bodies, and for whom that is the best they can do)—these people are slaves by nature, and it is better for them to be subject to this kind of control, and it is better for the other creatures I have mentioned. For a man who is able to belong to another person is by nature a slave (for that is why he belongs to someone else) . . . Assistance regarding the necessities of life is provided by both groups,

A slave's tombstone in a churchyard cemetery

by slaves and by domestic animals. Nature must therefore have intended to make the bodies of free men and of slaves different also; slaves' bodies strong for the services they have to do, those of free men upright and not much use for that kind of work, but instead useful for community life.[59]

In 1832, John P. Kennedy published a widely read novel, *Swallow Barn*, whose narrator was supposed to be from the liberal North. The narrator visits a plantation in Virginia expecting to see all manner of horrors perpetrated upon those whom he presupposes are the miserable victims of slavery. But, (and what an enlightening experience!) he finds only, in the words of Sterling Brown, "a kindly patriarchy and grateful, happy slaves."[60] Kennedy's narrator croons,

> I am sure they could never become a happier people than I find here . . . No tribe of people has ever passed from bar-barism to civilization whose progress has been more secure from harm, more genial to their character, or better sup-plied with mild and beneficent guardianship, adapted to the actual state of their intellectual feebleness, than the Negroes of Swallow Barn. And from what I can gather, it is pretty much the same on the other estates in this region.[61]

Similarly, a worker in an egg "factory" revealed parallel attitudes to me in the course of an interview I conducted with her. The conditions in the area where the chickens were housed were so abhorrent that I had to go outside every few minutes to breathe. Dust and ammonia filled the air, as the excrement pit beneath the rows and rows of cages holding the "laying-hens" was emptied only once every two years. The chickens were living four-to-a-cage a little larger than the size of a record album cover, and had been de-beaked, a process in which part of their upper mandibles are cut off. They lived in these conditions for two years until they were moved into trucks—their first and only experience of the outdoors—and driven to a slaughter-house. Below is a portion of my conversation with the worker:

Q: Do you think about the chickens much?

A: Usually I don't... The chickens here... know where their next meal is coming from, and they don't have to worry about predators...

Q: It seems like a lot of their natural tendencies are inhibited though, in terms of expression, a pecking order, being able to mate...

A: Well, no, they don't mate. They do, oh... they stretch; and they're happy. We see them, when we're walking through the place removing the dead... and they stretch. The pecking order: I think they have it in their individual cages.

Q: Well, not being able to walk, or turn around, or scratch...

A: Well on the other hand, if we were to put them out on the floor, it would take a lot more labor to gather the eggs. And eggs would cost a great deal more.

Q: But in terms of the chickens who are doing the actual work, producing the eggs. What would they be happier with?

A: On the other hand, what's the alternative? Do we quit eating eggs?

Q: Why do you have to de-beak them?

A: The chickens will, in their pecking order, pick on the weakest chicken... Once they draw blood, then they just keep on going. They're quite cannibalistic.

Q: But when they're in a barnyard that usually doesn't happen.

A: No, but then the one who's being picked on can get away.

*Swallow Barn* was intentionally written as a pro-slavery propaganda piece, whereas the comments of the egg-worker show how thoroughly a person is able to *internalize* propaganda. While the novel hoped to convince those who had *never visited* a plantation of the idyllic life led by plantation slaves, the interview reveals how it is possible to be daily confronted with reality, yet cease to see it.

What is at work here in both these instances is an attempt to brush over a potentially unsettling reality; to cease to hear the cries of our slaves, to believe that their spilt blood means something different from our own, and, finally, to believe that not only is the bondage we impose upon our slaves not a hindrance to them, but that it is a benefit.

In his book *The Pursuit of Loneliness: American Culture at the Breaking Point*, sociologist Philip Slater describes a pattern of thought which he terms "The Toilet Assumption,"

> the notion that unwanted matter, unwanted difficulties, unwanted complexities and obstacles will disappear if they're removed from our immediate field of vision . . .

He continues:

> Our approach to social problems is to decrease their visibility. This is the real foundation of racial segregation, especially in its most extreme case, the Indian "reserva-

tion." The result of our social efforts has been to remove the underlying problems of our society farther and farther from daily experiences and daily consciousness, and hence to decrease in the mass of the population, the knowledge, skill, and motivation necessary to deal with them.[62]

Whether we defend the violation of another's life through our denial of a reality which makes us uncomfortable, or through outright enthusiasm for oppressive power relations, the results are devastating. Such dynamics allow us to perpetuate and escalate actions which prevent others from pursuing their own destinies. Thus it is that we can happily bring our children to the zoo, to see the animals permanently displayed there, and believe that their comparatively barren, uni-dimensional existences might mimic the wild, that their dearly-gained "security" might compensate for their almost fathomless lost freedom—a freedom doubly, irretrievably, lost because beyond the walls and cages of the zoo we are permitting the irrevocable destruction of their natural habitats. It is noteworthy that even as recently as 1906, the New York Zoological Society displayed an African Pygmy, named Ota Benga, in a cage with chimpanzees.[63]

The pattern of thought described so insightfully by Slater—and which is so necessary for those who wish to simply ignore the myriad problems and suffering inherent to oppression—is also an integral requirement for the maintenance and perpetuation of the secrecy which surrounds the machinery of oppression. The next chapter will explore this secrecy.

> If you do not see the victims of cruelty and can explain cruelty away and live with the destruction comfortably, you are adrift . . .
>
> —Philip P. Hallie, *Cruelty*

# SECRECY: HIDING FROM THE TRUTH

Institutional cruelty does everything it can to conceal the fact that it is destroying its victims, and in doing this it keeps its spectators from feeling disgust and from being confused by the paradox of trying to justify the unjustifiable, of trying to praise the smashing of the weak.

—Philip P. Hallie, *Cruelty*

In the institutionalized cruelty of black slavery in the United States, secrecy was maintained, explains Hallie, by way of "isolated plantations, and later [after the abolition] by xenophobic little communities that jealously concealed from the outside world any facts about the way they treated their black people."[64]

Segregation was another apparatus by which a complex and disturbing social reality was concealed from members of society. For some—the die-hard racists—segregation allowed a continuation of the myth of white superiority by eliminating the possibility of normal day-to-day contact between the races, which, if it occurred, would inevitably point to equality between them. For those others who were not actively racist, segregation served to forestall "unpleasant" awakenings into the gross disparities between the economic and educational situations and opportunities of the two races.

Secrecy serves to conceal the details of the horror from all but those who must participate in it to keep the cogs of the machinery running smoothly. In the case of blacks, those participants in the system included the slave owners, dealers, and hunters in the antebellum period, as well as many in the postbellum era, such as owners of stores and restaurants serving blacks, owners of the buildings in which they lived, owners of the land they worked, police and sheriffs, and many others. In effect, segregation served to keep those outside the system blind to almost everything that institutionalized inequality entailed.

This same technique was used in Nazi Germany. Long before the mass killing of Jews actually began, a succession of restrictive laws were enacted, which served to segregate Jews away from the rest of the German population, in both the physical and social sense. Non-Jews were forbidden to speak to Jews, even in the case of a long-standing prior friendship. This was necessary to reduce people's understanding of, and empathy for, Jewish people, a prerequisite for mass extermination. This way, whatever happened to the Jews was out of the line of peoples' moral vision.

Secrecy and distancing are also used to protect the very profitable institutionalized cruelty to animals as it exists today. Vivisection laboratories and other facilities are notoriously difficult to enter. In most cases it is impossible for a citizen to enter without breaking the law. Even veterinarians can be denied admittance, and law-enforcement agents are not permitted to enter without a search warrant, which is difficult to obtain without evidence of wrong-doing. And yet one cannot gather the necessary evidence without first gaining access to a lab.

Likewise, the public is not generally admitted to the windowless "factory farm" buildings, each an isolated plantation in itself, which are scattered in out-of-the-way locations across the country. On a single farm one might find ten windowless

An enslaved man in a spike collar to limit movement and contact

Rabbit immobilized for eye-irritancy tests

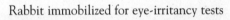

structures, each holding 70,000 chickens whose entire existences have been reduced to egg production. Or one might find dairy cows or pigs in these buildings, as it is becoming common to house both of these animals indoors for the duration of their lives. Slaughterhouses, despite the mandatory presence of U.S.D.A. inspectors, are also closed to public scrutiny.

All of this secrecy is necessary to keep the system intact. In the case of animal slavery, the outsiders are not mere spectators, as Hallie described, but are complicit in the system; nearly everyone quite literally feeds upon the fruits of this cruelty. And in order to be able to go on doing so, in order to avoid change in our lives or habits—which might be the inevitable result of a sober appraisal of the established system—we must participate in perpetuating our own ignorance of reality. We must be able to disassociate the actual producers—the animals themselves—from their "products:" fur, meat, milk, eggs, etc. Or we must be able to pretend that everyone is happy down on the farm, and smile, as we purchase that carton of milk, to picture a happy cow frolicking with her calf in a field. When buying what is euphemistically termed "beef," the consumer must picture, if *anything*, a large beefy brainless sort of creature who doesn't even have the sense to notice he's alive.

But what of those who are not mere spectators, complicit in their silence, but are active participants, willfully committing violence against others? While the spectator participates in the system through his or her inaction (and support as a consumer of the products of exploitation), the participation of these individuals is in the realm of action. These are the people who hold the scalpels, wear the white hoods, wield the whips, and in whose pockets are the keys to the chains and shackles. The next chapters will explore why they have come to commit their violence and crave control over others.

# PROFITS OVER ALL

The anti-slavery crusade,... the ranting of a handful of moralistic bigots, [which attempted]... to abolish so very important and necessary a branch of commercial interest, must have been crushed at once had not the insignificance of the zealots who vainly took the lead in it, made the vast body of planters, merchants and others, whose immense properties were involved in the trade... suppose that there would be no danger.
— James Boswell, *The Life of Samuel Johnson*, 1791

It is not difficult to appreciate that a cow's udder is highly important to a great industry and even to the welfare of the peoples of the world.
— YAPP, *Dairy Cattle*[65]

Part and parcel of attempts to justify slavery, and to obfuscate its existence in the eyes of spectators, are the motives for doing so. On a personal and societal level, monetary gain can be implicated as quite a motivator. To a large extent, the heightened *institutionalization* of oppression of blacks (in the form of legalized slavery), and animals (in factory farming and vivisection), can be attributed to the profit-motive. Indeed, eighteenth- and nineteenth-century anti-abolitionists contended that the end of slavery would bring with it the collapse of the economic structure of the Southern United States, while in our own century C.W. Hume wrote that "the major cruelties practiced on animals in civilized countries today arise out of commercial exploitation, and the fear of losing profits is the chief obstacle to reform.[66]

Certainly it is true that a fear of competition and dwindling profits may be responsible for a farmer's decision to automate his egg production system and tight-pack more birds into fewer cages. As others in the industry force their animals to produce more, an individual farmer is often economically beleaguered, if only by the bank, into following accordingly. But it is only possible for him to increase pressure on his chickens if he has already mentally negated their existences

as individuals. He must already view them as lessers to himself, perhaps so much his lessers that he has denied the importance of their feelings, or actually can no longer think of them as having any feelings at all. To him they have become merely a means to his profitable end.

A person who owned a large number of slaves, but left them under the charge of an overseer, was in a similar situation. He could let the machinery (in this case the very human overseer) run its course, doing whatever was necessary to push the slaves toward maximum productivity without having to deal with them—in thought or action—as individuals.

These examples seem to point to a neat bundle of explanation: "slavery and oppression are created in the quest for profit." But we have already seen that there is more to the problem than this explanation would allow. Before the possibility of any profitability can be conceived of, the minds of those who will stand to profit must be ready to accept all that the oppressor/oppressed relationship will entail. For those so predisposed, a hazily understood version of evolutionary theory is all they need to avoid giving the lives of their victims another thought.

In the pre-Darwinian seventeenth, eighteenth, and nineteenth centuries, religion—Christianity, to be more precise—served a similar function. The Christian worldview regarded ("civilized" as opposed to "savage") humans as the beneficiaries of God's universe, the reason for which all else was created. A characteristic essay written in 1833 was entitled "On the Power, Wisdom, and Goodness of God as Manifested in the Adaptation of External Nature to the Moral and Intellectual Constitution of Man." Under the precepts of "Manifest Destiny," ruling all of God's creation with an iron fist found justification.

And later, by inverting evolutionary theory as Darwin had intended it, through a very minor but far-reaching adjustment, this attitude toward the rest of life on the planet could continue to be justified and rationalized. (This skewed vision and application of evolution *vis a vis* other humans was termed "Social Darwinism," discussed earlier.) So, despite the huge scandal the theory of evolution caused in Darwin's age—enraging the church and its leaders—with a quick twist in meaning and intent it was used to serve one of the same *purposes* as institutionalized religion once had: justifying the exploitation and oppression of others based on their differences. What was once "Manifest Destiny" became "Evolutionary Destiny." And, in the minds of many, we eventually saw the system of science supplant that of religion as a justifier of atrocities perpetrated upon others. The *purpose* hadn't changed, only the *masters*.

But has it really ever been very different throughout the history of Western culture? We have already seen Aristotle's detailed and enthusiastic explanations of slavery's justness. In a similar vein, interwoven with its laws for morally proscribed behavior, The Old Testament—Christianity's forebear—provides its readers with detailed instructions about one's relationships with slaves, with oxen, with one's wives and daughters.

According to Scripture, new laws delineating expected behavior were given Moses (in Exodus) directly by God. Most of us are quite familiar with the basic laws, which read, in part, "Thou shalt not covet thy neighbor's house. Thou shalt not covet thy neighbor's wife, nor his manservant, nor his maidservant, nor his ox . . . "[67] And further, "if the ox were wont to gore in time past, and warning hath been given to his owner, yet he hath not kept him in, and he killeth a man or a woman: the ox shall be stoned, and his owner also should of right be put to death.[68] . . . If any harm ensue, then thou shalt give life for life. Eye for eye, tooth for tooth, hand for hand, foot for foot. Burning for burning, wound for wound, bruise for bruise.[69]

86

While this was certainly not yet the God who would later enjoin us to "turn the other cheek," it was a God who at least made the punishment fit the crime, for the first time guaranteeing equal protection under the law. Yet on a closer reading, we see that some were more "equally" protected than others. If your ox killed a slave, according to Exodus 21:32, the ox was still stoned to death, but you weren't; you instead had to pay 30 shekels of silver to the slave's master. If you killed a man's ox, the penalty was the same as if you'd killed his manservant or maidservant, and you again paid in silver, not with your own life:[70]

Far from condemning slavery, the Ten Commandments, along with the Bible's four books full of laws, set forth detailed rules governing its practice and providing the comparative values of *all* of a man's chattel, be it his spouse, female children, livestock, or other slaves. You could sell your daughters into slavery without penalty, and if a master has given his slave a wife, who has borne him children, upon the slave's manumission "the wife and her children shall belong to her master, and he shall go out by himself."[71] Exodus 21 continues:

> And if the servant should plainly say, "I love my master, my wife, and my children; I will not go out free: Then shall his master bring him unto the judges, and he shall also bring him to the door, or unto the door-post; and his master shall bore his ear through with an awl; and he shall serve him till the jubilee [for life].[72]

But the laws set forth in the Bible do not end with proscribing behavior for interaction with merely the family and our own communities. Proper behavior was also delineated for interactions with peoples of other religions, who in biblical times were pagans—followers of an earth-based religion—and

87

considered to be godless savages and heathens. How little things change. Even then, God was to have condoned, even encouraged, the violent vanquishing of all those who were not his "chosen" people. Provisions were also made for taking all the material wealth of one's self-appointed adversaries. In the book of Numbers, God is said to have told Moses of his enemy, "Fear him not: for into thy hand have I delivered him, and all his people, and his land." And so "they smote him and his sons, and all his people, until there was none left alive... and they took possession of his land."[73]

In another conquest, "the children of Israel took captives the women of Midian, and their little ones: and all their cattle, and all their flocks, and all their goods, they took as spoil... And Moses said unto them, 'have ye allowed all the females to live?'" And because it was the surviving women of an earlier conquest of a pagan community who had evidently caused the children of Israel to disobey God, consequently bringing on a plague, Moses now declared that only young virgin

*above*, Wedgwood anti-slavery cameo, circa 1787; and on *facing page*, parody of the cameo as it appeared in *Punch*, 1861

females might be spared, to be taken for slaves and concubines. And of course, they also "took all the... cattle."[74] In Deuteronomy, it's back again to killing *all* the people, "devoted to destruction every city, the men, the women, and the little ones. But all the cattle, and the spoil of the cities," were taken as "booty."[75]

Charles Darwin, in a land-excursion during his travels aboard the H.M.S. *Beagle*, witnessed such biblical pursuits all over again, this time in Argentina's Patagonia region, where natives were being cleared from their land to make way for cattle ranching, much like the scenario in North America's Midwest. Upon seeing the slaughter of the Native Patagonians, Darwin attempted to convince the leader of the Argentine conquerors to at least spare the lives of the women (those who were not wanted for soldiers' concubines were to be killed along with all the men); he was rebuffed. As it was explained to him, "You can't keep them. They breed so fast." In brief, summarized a

MONKEYANA.

AM I A MAN AND A BROTHER?

biographer, Darwin was told "the Indians were vermin, worse than rats, and that was that."[76] Darwin confided to his diary that he thought the Christian soldiers to be much more savage than the helpless pagans they were destroying. (As for the system of slavery, Darwin shared the abolitionist sentiments of his cousins [and wife's family], the Wedgwood's, who actively campaigned to bring slavery to an end. "I thank God," he wrote after the conclusion of his journey on the *Beagle*, "I shall never again visit a slave country."[77])

The habit of claiming that God, or some higher order, has ordained our barbaric or avaricious practices is obviously not new; nor, quite obviously, is it outdated. When someone wants to take slaves, gold, land, someone else's cattle, or, for that matter, to draw a salary for administering electric shocks to infant rats, it is certainly convenient to say that God or Evolution makes it right.

But what still remains unexplained is the proclivity of the "civilized" human's psyche towards accepting the justification of oppression that Social Darwinism or some forms of religion have to offer. And this is the essence of our riddle, for we see that one system of justification is easily superseded by another, even when the new system—for example, Darwin's theory of evolution—should actually serve to *lessen* oppression. It seems that the desire to oppress others is so ingrained in many humans that they readily distort even a liberating theory or concept into its inverse, creating another wall of defense against positive change. Ultimately, an unbiased observer of human behavior must conclude that most action is not shaped by theory, but rather theories are shaped to conform to actions we have no intention of changing.

Throughout this book, and especially in the chapter on hunting, we began to examine the nature of power, and saw that this was perhaps much more crucial to our search for the roots of oppression and slavery than many of the other relevant issues we have explored. For while the profit motive serves to explain *some* aspects of vivisection, factory farming, and the black slave trade, it fails miserably at explaining, for example, lynching or segregation, or the calculated cruelty involved in many "scientific" experiments, or the joy many people derive from killing. Oppression is carried far beyond the point of profitability and mere economic exploitation.

To attempt to flatly arrive at *the* cause of humans' cruelty is to attempt the impossible. There is no more *one reason* for someone's cruelty towards another than there is *one manifestation* of that cruelty. What we can hope to do is explore several possible sources or motivators for cruel behavior, and through them form a sort of patchwork image of the face of human cruelty.

# POWER

The ox, as the Greeks used to say, was the poor man's slave; and even the poorest tinker had a dog at his heels on which to bestow the kick which indicated his superiority.
— Keith Thomas, *Man and the Natural World*

Often, when a person is ill-treated or relegated to a demeaning position in society, they will respond by venting their frustrations at someone whose societal position is even lower than their own. It is not rational; their violent action in no way serves as a retaliation towards their own oppressors. Historian Coral Lansbury explores this dynamic:

> Rather than being seen as an aberration of human nature, the torture and killing of animals permitted those who had no rights, no possibility of ever imposing their will upon [other humans], to demonstrate, often publicly, their strength and dominance. When men who were accustomed to being thrashed and abused could watch the chained bull harried by a pack of dogs, it was like seeing the authority of the master torn apart by the mob.[78]

Taking this concept one step further, we can see that by torturing or dominating a powerful animal, such as a bull, or a tiger in a big-game hunt, the oppressors feel, unconsciously, that they have destroyed those who held power over them. By destroying or tormenting the weak, such as a rabbit or a child, the oppressors *become* the master who has in turn tortured them, their own victims' helpless writhings echoing what they have so often felt. Temporarily replaced in the role of victim, these new reactive torturers ascend, momentarily in their own minds, to the social- or physical-power position of their own masters.

But this ascension is short-lived and ineffectual, for the rise to power is only in their own minds. Having dominated those who are proven to be much weaker than themselves, they have done nothing to upset the relationship which is the source of their problem: that between the master and themselves, the victims. And they are still as powerless in this regard as they were before becoming someone else's oppressor. As long as their anger is directed at an innocent instead of at the perpetrator of their own victimization, the cycle—once started—will only with great effort be broken. This dynamic provides insight into the mind of the serial murderer, the compulsive hunter, and the

"The brand mark of inferiority has been indelibly, irrevocably, irretrievably, and. eternally impressed by the Creator upon the Negro, and... nothing can erase or obliterate it."
—John Campbell
*Negromania*, 1851

A harp seal is beaten to death for its fur

"And the fear of you and the dread of you shall be upon
every beast of the earth, and upon every fowl of the air,
upon all that moveth upon the earth, and upon all the
fishes of the sea; into your hands they are delivered."
—The Bible, Genesis 9:2.

93

violent offender. They cannot torture or murder enough of those who are weaker, though they turn to this occupation obsessively. For as hard as they may try to wipe out their oppressor, they are only doing it symbolically, which ultimately never works. A new symbol springs forth as the last gasps its final breath, and the lust for blood and power is never sated. These victim/oppressors may not even be actively dominated by another individual. They may be the slowly crushed victims of an inequitable economic system, or even suffering from the unresolved emotional wounds of a childhood which has long since passed.

In *Pornography and Silence*, Susan Griffin explores the deep roots of cruel behavior in human beings. Her terms "fascist" and "chauvinist" are used to denote anyone who engages in prejudicial and oppressive behavior towards others. From the following excerpt from her book, we see that her paradigm easily extends to include the racist and the speciesist:

> Far from experiencing nature directly, or as part of himself, the fascist mystifies natural knowledge. In this way he imagines himself to have been conferred with a special dispensation by nature, which paradoxically places him above nature.
>
> Thus the chauvinist confers upon himself the right to manipulate nature. He uses natural power to control his enemy. He transforms the natural experience of this other into an experience of helplessness, terror, and pain. He uses nature as an instrument of revenge against those...he has chosen as a symbol for his natural self...In the pornographer's world, therefore, sexual coitus, a most natural act, becomes an act of aggression, rape and violence. And it is no accident that for the prisoner of the Nazi concentration camp, every natural

impulse—hunger, thirst, the need to defecate, even to swallow, or to sleep—became another form of suffering, the basis for ridicule, or a means of torture.

By manipulating nature in this way, the chauvinist can control his experience of nature. Because he projects a dis-owned self on the other, whom, vicariously, he tortures with nature, he can experience his own fear of nature. (And at the same time he can prove to himself the truth of his conviction that nature is terrible, that nature is sadistic.)[79]

This model affords us new insight into the minds of the white colonists, driven to destroy and civilize wilderness; turn darkness into light; control the herbivorous animals of the forest while destroying the carnivores—over whom domination could not be as complete and whose predatory behavior (which resonated more closely with our own than did the behavior of herbivores) terrified the colonists. In 1707, for instance, Cotton Mather warned of "the *Evening Wolves*, the rabid and howling *Wolves* of the *Wilderness* [who] would make . . . Havock among you, *and not leave the Bones till the morning*."[80] Roderick Nash notes that "legends and folktales from the first contact until well into the national period linked the New World wilderness with a host of monsters, witches, and similar supernatural beings."[81]

In the colonists' terrified delusional state, these fears of supernatural forces were blended with a fear of very real and natural beings until all took on the glow of the netherworld, real and unreal alike. These irrational fears can be said to be born of a fear of what is sometimes termed "the darkness within," itself a racially-loaded phrase. People who dislike or are afraid of elements within themselves, such as strong emotion, sexual feelings, weakness, or violent urges, repress even their

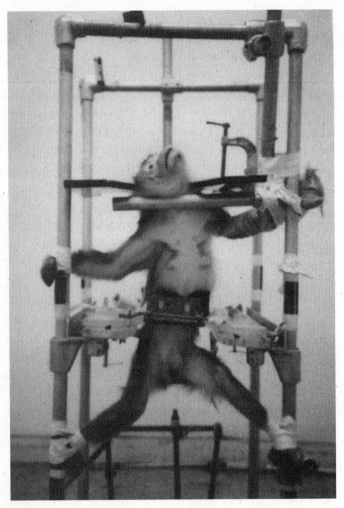

A monkey in a laboratory

"So far as I can see, unless one is initially prepared to adopt a rather rampant anthropomorphism in respect to animals, they can have no rights."
— R.G. Frey, *Interests and Rights: The Case Against Animals*, 1980

A pilloried slave

"Negroes have no rights which the white man is
bound to respect."
—Chief Justice Roger B. Taney,
member of the Supreme Court which
heard the Dred Scott Case

own knowledge of these parts of themselves. Really, then, what I have termed "irrational fears" are actually a fear of the so-called "irrational" part of one's own self. People deny these elements, yet at the same time want or need to know them, so they are projected onto someone or something else: women, black people, Jews, animals, or even Nature *herself*. Then, because these beings have now come to represent something of which this person is afraid, or cannot understand, or wants to deny in himself, the torture or perhaps even eradication of the symbol is enacted.

Thus we see Southern white men, for whom the rape of black women was not uncommon, portraying *black* men as rapists of white women. We see humans, themselves engaging in wars (often as a result of this same sort of delusional fear), and perpetrators of slavery and other injustices to humans, justifying their wholesale violence towards non-human animals on the grounds that "animals are incapable of distinguishing moral from immoral behavior." Through violent actions towards the symbol, the oppressors unconsciously try to destroy those qualities in themselves which they find so threatening and wish to deny. And this is why the actions, justifications, and even language of oppression are so similar even when the victims are, in some ways, so very different. This is one reason why the outward expressions of the oppression of blacks and animals have been so similar; to the powerful oppressor, all victims are all too similar. They are a part of the oppressor's own self reflected back to the oppressor. The victims are not seen as autonomous beings.

And this relates as well to the oppressor/oppressed relationship we first examined in this section: that of the oppressed *becoming* the oppressor. For the person who experiences life as a victim merely projects different qualities on his own would-be victims, and forces them to suffer the pain and degradation which he has experienced at the hands of his own master.

But these delusional plays are not acted out only in the minds of isolated individuals. They operate on a much larger societal level, with society serving to indoctrinate its members into its macro-mindset. Thus the fears and inhibitions which are peculiar to a given society are conveyed to and impressed upon its members often from birth, leading them, as we have seen, to play out society's pathological games on an individual level.

In 1965, Robert Wernick, a correspondent to the *Saturday Evening Post* declared the wilderness to be:

> . . . the dark, the formless, the terrible, the old chaos which our fathers pushed back. . . It is held at bay by constant vigilance, and when the vigilance slackens it swoops down for a melodramatic revenge.[82]

This passage encapsulates much of our society's formula for relating to "the other" which is really ourself. We can imagine the author to be speaking interchangeably of the black race; of the natural progression of plant-life as it "threatens" to re-establish itself in a cleared forest area; of the nature and spirit of a dog or horse who (but for our constant vigilance) might revert to their unbroken state; or of the woman accused of possession by devils. Blacks, animals, nature, women, Jews, and others have all been associated with the above sentiments, and with this paranoid imagery has come prejudicial treatment and oppression. And let us again consider the term "breaking-in." We associate wildness and freedom with chaos, whereas someone who is literally *broken* is civilized and thus a positive figure. That which is under our control, even if it is dead, *even if it must be killed*, is positive, while that which retains autonomy is threatening and negative.

In the Bible, Eve is led into temptation by a snake (an animal) and life in the civilized Garden of Eden comes to an

Masthead of *The Liberator*, the abolitionist newspaper started by William Lloyd Garrison in 1831

end; Adam and Eve are banished to the dangerous wilderness. And Adam's only downfall was being led astray by Eve. Within this paradigm, the white, male, human has projected all of his guilt, weakness, and desire for sinful acts onto a woman and an animal. And it is these two, along with the terrible wilderness and all those associated with it (let us not forget the "Prince of Darkness") who will continue to be the reflective surfaces onto which are projected the innermost fears, desires, and insecurities of human beings. When the *Saturday Evening Post* correspondent wrote of "the old chaos which our fathers pushed back," he would never have guessed that he was giving us an insight into the chaos—their denied and confused selves—which "our fathers" have been interminably struggling to push back into the unknown corners of their unconscious minds.

With this deeper understanding of what motivates people to oppress others, we are perhaps better equipped to see through attempts at justification made by the victimizers. We might now begin to test and understand, for example, the conflicting statements made by the vivisector about the nature of his victims. On the one hand, it is said that the animals are so *unlike us*

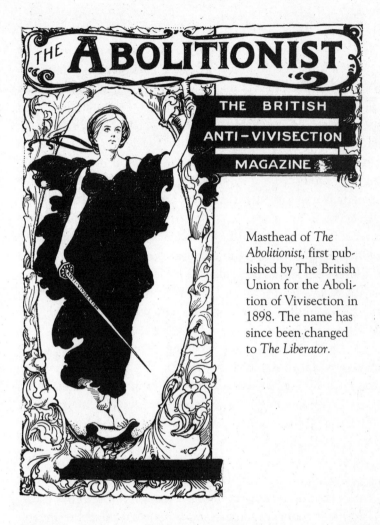

Masthead of *The Abolitionist*, first published by The British Union for the Abolition of Vivisection in 1898. The name has since been changed to *The Liberator*.

that they are not worthy of our consideration. On the other hand, vivisectors claim that animals are so *like us* that they are essential to research. In these conflicting statements we see a researcher's own confusion as to the genuine nature of his "subjects," and their nature in relation to his own.

We might also begin to see how we have allowed ourselves, both as a society and as individuals, to become intoxicated by such "confusion," and how obscure reality can become as a result. We can look at a child who has wantonly stoned a kitten to death, or is found coolly and carefully dismembering little creatures, and know that something is terribly, frighteningly, wrong with him. Yet when an adult "professional" does even worse—sewing the eyes of newborn kittens shut, or performing surgery on paralyzed yet unanesthetized animals (the former a documented experiment, the latter a common procedure)—we can't accept it for what it is. We instead believe what we are told: that we lack the ability to understand *what* is being done (and lacking that understanding cannot be allowed to see); and that there is a grand reason, also mysterious to us, why it *must* be done (that it is *only* through such actions that humans [or science, or commerce] will ever possibly manage to advance).

We must beware of those who seek to convince us that their deeds of violence towards others are necessitated by the "common good." No matter how noble the oppressors claim to be, we must remember that the infliction of pain and suffering becomes a pleasurable act, an end in itself. Coral Lansbury explores the all-too-commonplace mechanics of sadism:

> That cruelty can be extraordinarily satisfying cannot be denied, for cruelty is the magnifier of identity, a simplifier of social function, and the temporary resolution of insecurity and doubt... Cruelty relies upon a rigid observance of the categorical distance between victim and oppressor.[83]

Turn-of-the-century anti-vivisectionist Frances Cobbe also remarked upon the pleasure some derive from committing acts of cruelty. Lansbury presents Cobbe's argument that:

vivisectors had fallen victim to *Schadenfreude*, that most insidious form of wickedness, a delight in the spectacle of pain. The students watching an animal contorted with agony in a laboratory were responding in the same fashion as the crowd around the cockpit [the arena used in cockfights] or bullring, and that it was disingenuous to claim otherwise... [84]

*"Schadenfreude,"* concludes Lansbury about Cobbe's observations, "... could take many different forms, from flogging children and wife beating to tormenting animals in the name of science."[85]

To those who would be master, what matters is not so much *who* their slaves will be, but that there are slaves to be had. As one group becomes off-bounds due to changing laws or the tide of social change, attention will be turned to a different weak group, or focussed more intensely upon a prior class of victims. But even this shift comes begrudgingly, for the oppressors have come to enjoy their cruel pleasures. The most important things to masters, therefore, is that the public will not become cognizant of what is being done—often in its name—and that public opinion will not turn against them, thus depriving them of their slaves.

In order to prevent these two events from occurring, masters have built into society a long succession of supposed defenses and justifications for systems of oppression and slavery, designed to confound the public into complacency. And masters have done everything in their power to hide the very fact that oppression was and is taking place, knowing that secrecy is the best protection of their power.

Returning to Slater's notion of "The Toilet Assumption," we see that this secrecy cannot be maintained for very long unless potential witnesses wish to ignore reality. For those Germans living in the surrounding areas of Nazi death camps with their crematoriums, it must have taken a lot of energy to *avoid* realizing (as they claimed) that the endless black clouds streaming out of the immense smokestacks were actually the ashes of murdered people. Similarly, South African President Botha's media blackout, instated in 1985, did little to hide the events in his country, except from those people who *chose* not to comprehend the obvious realities.

As more of us examine the cultural prejudices of our society—and the prejudices of our species—we begin to unravel the traditions, institutions, and actions of the master mentality. It is at times a painful path, as we discover in ourselves some of the beliefs and feelings that we had, in different circumstances, perhaps disdained in others. But, ultimately, it is a path promising hope and the possibility for a future of peace—something we have almost stopped hoping for. With every new perspective gained, doors open to the world that afford us greater depth of experience and existence. The realization that the animals we enslave, the animals we treat as *things*, the animals who slave for us, are *alive*, are as possessive of their lives as you or I, this realization drastically changes one's perspective. Hopefully, it will also change our actions. And we may, in discovering the others with whom we share this earth, discover even more of ourselves.

> It is only by the spread of the same democratic spirit that animals can enjoy the "rights" for which even [humans] have for so long struggled in vain. The emancipation of [humans] from cruelty and injustice will bring with it in due course the emancipation of animals also. The two reforms are inseparably connected, and neither can be fully realized alone.
> —Henry Salt, 1894

# AFTERWORD
## TO THE REVISED EDITION

Traditional Native American peoples thought generationally, seeing themselves, as individuals and communities, as part of a long and continuing chain of tradition and experience. Some tribes had oral histories, chronicling important events, reaching back hundreds of years. In contrast to this, in our culture today we tend to live in the absolute present, having very little connection to things which happened fifty, fifteen, or even five years ago; the events, thoughts, and feelings of 100 or 200 years ago seem ancient history—done and felt by distant ghosts.

And yet we, like the Native Americans, share in our ancestors' heritage. The violence which we today perpetrate upon animals and upon the earth is the same violence of two hundred years prior. The victims may change; some may cease to be societally-sanctioned as we move along in our cultural evolution. But we delude ourselves to think that the heart of today's "master" beats very differently from that of his or her forebears.

Far beyond the identity of the victims, violence and oppression have existed as a continuum throughout the history of our culture. Even lacking overt societal approval, violent behavior towards individuals or groups nevertheless continues. And so it shall, until we break the cycle of this behavior. For ultimately, while the pathological psychological, social, and institutional framework for oppressive and violent behavior remains, laws can do little more than push that behavior behind closed doors, or beneath the immediately apparent surface.

If we are to succeed in stemming our destructiveness and learning to once again live sustainably and harmoniously with the earth and all of its inhabitants, it is the urge to commit violence that must be addressed—both on a societal level, and, perhaps most importantly, in ourselves as individuals.

Ultimately, the true battle against oppression will be waged within each of us, because that is where all violence begins. And that is also the only place where violence—with enough work—can finally, everlastingly, be brought to an end.

# WHAT OTHERS HAVE SAID

There is no denying that slavery had a direct and positive tendency to produce coarseness and brutality in the treatment of animals, especially those most useful to agricultural industry. Not only the slave, but the horse, the ox and the mule shared the general feeling of indifference to the right naturally engendered by a state of slavery. The master blamed the overseer, the overseer the slave, and the slave the horses, oxen and mules, and violence fell upon the animals as a consequence.

—Frederick Douglass, (1817-1895)

I and my daughters and husband have been regarded as almost fanatical in our care of animals wherever we have been, and in Florida we have seen much to affect us; not so much in the oppression of the useful animals, as in the starving of other creatures which people keep and will not feed. Again we have been distressed by the wholesale barbarity of tourists who seem to make Florida animals mere marks for unskillful hunters to practice upon, and who go everywhere maiming, wounding and killing poor birds and beasts that they do not even stop to pick up, and shoot in mere wantonness. Last year we exerted ourselves to get a law passed protecting the birds of Florida which were being trapped and carried off by thousands to die in miserable little cages... veritable slave ships... I for my part am ready to do anything that can benefit the cause.

—Harriet Beecher Stowe, author of
*Uncle Tom's Cabin*, from letter, 6 November 1877

...The philosophy of nonviolence which I had learned from Dr. Martin Luther King Jr., during my involvement in the civil rights movement, was first responsible for my change in diet.

I became a vegetarian in 1965. I had been a participant in all of the "major" and most of the "minor" civil rights demonstrations of the early sixties, including the March on Washington and the Selma to Montgomery March. Under the leadership of Dr. King, I became totally committed to nonviolence, and I was convinced that nonviolence meant opposition to killing in any form. I felt the commandment "Thou shalt not kill" applied to human beings not only in their dealings with each other—war, lynching, assassination, murder and the like—but in their practice of killing animals for food and sport. Animals and humans suffer and die alike. Violence causes the same pain, the same spilling of blood, the same stench of death, the same arrogant, cruel and brutal taking of life.

One night... I made the decision never to eat meat again. I had become firmly convinced that the killing of animals for food was both immoral and unnatural.

> —Dick Gregory, *Dick Gregory's Natural Diet*
> *For Folks Who Eat*, 1973

Animals, whom we have made our slaves, we do not like to consider our equal.

> —Charles Darwin, (1809-1882)

I think the rapidly growing tendency to regard animals as born for nothing except slavery to so-called humanity absolutely disgusting.

> —Sir Victor Gollancz, (1893-1967), *The Unlived Life*

It should be the study of every farmer to make his horse his companion and friend, and to do this, there is but one rule, and that is, uniform sympathy and kindness. All loud and boisterous commands, a brutal flogging should be banished from the field, and only words of cheer and encouragement should be tolerated. A horse is in many respects like a man. He has five senses, and has memory, affection, and reason...
—Frederick Douglass, (1817-1895)

I am in favor of animal rights as well as human rights. That is the way of a whole human being.
—Abraham Lincoln, (1809-1865), *Complete Works*

...So de white man throw down de load and tell de nigger man tuh pick it up. He hand it to his womanfolks. De nigger woman is de mule uh de world so fur as Ah can see...
—Zora Neale Hurston, *Their Eyes Were Watching God*, 1937

(Animals are) those unfortunate slaves and victims of the most brutal part of mankind.
—John Stuart Mill, 1868

At one time the benevolent affections embrace merely the family, soon the circle expanding includes first a class, then a nation, then a coalition of nations, then all humanity; and finally its influence is felt in the dealing of [humans] with the animal world. In each of these cases a standard is formed different from that of the preceding stage, but in each case the same tendency is recognized as a virtue.
—W.E.H. Lecky, *The History of European Morals*, 1869

In December of 1986, three black men sought to use a telephone in a Queens, New York pizza parlor after their car broke down. A mob formed and, encouraged by exhortations to "get the niggers" grabbed baseball bats and a tree limb and chased the men through the streets of Howard Beach, Queens. One escaped, one was severely beaten, and the third, Michael Griffith, in a desperate attempt to escape, ran onto the Belt Parkway. Here he was hit by the car of Dominick Blum—the son of a policeman—and thrown onto the hood of the automobile. Blum did not bother to stop to investigate, reportedly later telling police he thought he had hit "an animal." To complete the picture, then-New York Mayor Koch commented that "the survivors were chased like animals through the streets, with one of them being killed on the highway."

—As reported in *The New York Times*[86]

To the casual reader, some of the writing of Mark Twain has appeared to be both anti-animal and racist. This is, however, far from being true. Twain was a skilled satirist, and this, combined with his ability to write so convincingly in the voice of others, led to some grave misunderstandings regarding his intentions. In the excerpt below, we listen in on a conversation between Thorndike and Antonio, two army scouts on the frontier, as Antonio prepares to return to Spain, and see that not only was Twain outraged by the treatment of, and attitudes towards, both blacks and animals, but that he also felt that when people who delight in cruelty towards one group, it often follows that they delight in cruelty to another. —M.S.

"I wish I was going, Antonio. There's two things I'd give a lot to see. One's a railroad. . . The other's a bullfight."

"I've seen lots of them; I wish I could see another."

"I don't know anything about it, except in a mixed-up foggy way, Antonio, but I know enough to know it's a grand sport."

"The grandest in the World! There's no other sport that begins with it. I'll tell you what I've seen, then you can judge. It was my first, and it's as vivid to me now as it was when I saw it. It was a Sunday afternoon, and beautiful weather, and my uncle, the priest, took me as a reward for being a good boy and because of my own accord and without anybody asking me I had bankrupted my savings-box and given the money to a mission that was civilizing the Chinese and sweetening their lives and softening their hearts with the gentle teachings of our religion, and I wish you could have seen what we saw that day, Thorndike."

"The amphitheater was packed, from the bull ring to the highest row—twelve thousand people in one circling mass, one slanting, solid mass—royalties, nobles, clergy, ladies, gentlemen, state officials, generals, admirals, soldiers, sailors, lawyers, thieves, merchants, brokers, cooks, housemaids, scullery-maids, doubtful women, dudes, gamblers, beggars, loafers, tramps, American ladies, gentlemen, preachers, English. . . German. . . French. . . all the world represented: Spaniards to admire and praise, foreigners to enjoy and go home and find fault—there they were, one solid, sloping, circling sweep of rippling and flashing color under the downpour of the summer sun—just a garden, a gaudy gorgeous flower garden! Children munching oranges, six thousand fans fluttering and glimmering. . . lovely girl-faces smiling recognition and salutation to other lovely girl-faces, gray old ladies and gentlemen dealing in the like exchanges with each other—ah, such a picture of cheery contentment and glad anticipation! not a mean spirit, nor a sordid soul, nor a sad heart there—ah, Thorndike, I wish I could see it again."

"Suddenly, the martial note of a bugle cleaves the hum and murmur—clear the ring!"

"They clear it. The great gate is flung open, and the procession marches in, splendidly costumed and glittering: the marshals of the day, then the picadores on horseback, then the matadores on foot, each surrounded by his quadrille of *chulos*. They march to the box of the city fathers, and formally salute. The key is thrown, the bull gate is unlocked. Another bugle blast—the gate flies open, the bull plunges in, furious, trembling, blinking in the blinding light, and stands there, a magnificent creature, center of those multitudinous and admiring eyes . . . He sees his enemy: horsemen sitting motionless, with long spears in rest, upon blindfolded broken-down nags, lean and starved, fit only for sport and sacrifice, then the carrion heap."

"The bull makes a rush with murder in his eye, but a picador meets him with a spear-thrust in the shoulder. He flinches in pain, and the picador skips out of danger. A burst of applause for the picador, hisses for the bull. Some shout 'Cow!' at the bull and call him offensive names. But he is not listening to them, he is there for business; he is not minding the cloak-bearers that come fluttering around to confuse him; he chases this way, he chases that way, and hither and yon, scattering the nimble banderillos in every direction like a spray, and receiving their maddening darts in his neck as they dodge and fly—oh but it is a lively spectacle and brings down the house! Ah, you should hear the thundering roar that goes up when the game is at its wildest and brilliant things are done!"

"Oh, that first bull, that day, was great! From the moment the spirit of war rose to flood-tide in him and he got down to his work, he began to do wonders. He tore his way through his persecutors, flinging one of them clear over the parapet; he bowled a horse and his rider down, and plunged straight for the next, got home with his horns, wounding both horse and man; on again, here and there this way and that; and one after another he tore the bowels out of two horses so that they gushed to the ground, and ripped a third one so badly that although they rushed him

112

to cover and shoved his bowels back and stuffed the rents with tow and rode him against the bull again, he couldn't make the trip; he tried to gallop, under the spur, but soon reeled and tottered and fell, all in a heap. For a while, that bull-ring was the most thrilling and glorious and inspiring sight that was ever seen. The bull absolutely cleared it, and stood there alone! monarch of the place. The people went mad for pride in him, and joy and delight, and you couldn't hear yourself think, for the roar and boom and crash of applause."

"Antonio, it carries me clear out of myself to hear you tell it . . . If I live, I'll see a bullfight yet before I die. Did they kill him?"

"Oh, yes, that is what the bull is for. They tired him out, and got him at last. He kept rushing the matador, who always slipped smartly and gracefully aside in time, waiting for a sure chance; and at last it came; the bull made a deadly plunge for him—was avoided neatly, and as he sped by, the long sword glided silently into him, between his left shoulder and spine—in and in, to the hilt. He crumpled down, dying."

"Ah Antonio, it *is* the noblest sport that ever was. I would give a year of my life to see it. Is the bull always killed?"

"Yes. Sometimes a bull is timid, finding himself in so strange a place, and he stands trembling, or tries to retreat. Then everybody despises him for his cowardice and wants him punished and made ridiculous; so they hough him from behind, and it is the funniest thing in the world to see him hobbling around on severed legs; the whole vast house goes into hurricanes of laughter over it; I have laughed till the tears ran down my cheeks to see it. When he has furnished all the sport he can, he is not any longer useful, and is killed."

"Well, it is perfectly grand, Antonio, perfectly beautiful. Burning a nigger don't begin." .

—Mark Twain, from "A Horse's Tale," 1906

# FURTHER READING

## NATURE AND ANIMALS

*THEM*, Marjorie Spiegel, (Mirror Books, 1998).

*The Secret Life of Plants*, (1989), & *Secrets of the Soil*, (1990), Peter Tompkins & Christopher Bird, (both Harper & Row).

*When Elephants Weep: The Emotional Lives of Animals*, Jeffrey Moussaieff Masson and Susan McCarthy, (Delacorte, 1995).

*The Man Who Planted Trees*, Jean Giono, (Chelsea Green, 1985).

*A Brief History of Time*, Stephen Hawking, (Bantam, 1988).

*Natural Creation & The Formative Mind*, John Davidson, (Element Books, 1991).

*Living Earth Manual of Feng Shui*, Stephen Skinner (Arkana, 1982).

*Woman and Nature*, Susan Griffin, (Harper & Row, 1979).

*The Hidden Life of Dogs*, (Pocket Books, 1995), & *The Tribe of Tiger*, (Touchstone, 1994), by Elizabeth Marshall Thomas.

*The Old Brown Dog: Women, Workers and Vivisection in Edwardian England*, Coral Lansbury, (University of Wisconsin, 1985).

*Silent Spring*, Rachel Carson. Reprint. (Houghton Mifflin, 1994).

*Sacred Elephant, Whale Nation*, and *Falling for a Dolphin*, all by Heathcote Williams, (out of print in the U.S.).

## African-American Studies

*From Slavery to Freedom: A History*, John Hope Franklin, ed., (Knopf, 1994).

*Narrative of the Life of Frederick Douglass*, Frederick Douglass. Reprint. (Dover, 1995).

*Race Matters*, Cornel West, (Vintage, 1994).

*African American Literature: Voices in a Tradition*, An Anthology by Holt, Rinehart & Winston, (Harcourt Brace, 1992).

*Black Voices: An Anthology of Afro-American Literature*, Abraham Chapman, ed., (Penguin Books, 1968).

*Age, Race, Class and Sex*, Angela Davis, (Vintage, 1983).

*Ain't I a Woman: Black Women and Feminism*, bell hooks, (South End Press, 1981).

*Souls of Black Folks*, W.E.B. DuBois, (Signet, 1969).

*Things Fall Apart*, Chinua Achiebe, (Anchor Books, 1959).

*Another Country*, James Baldwin, (Farrar, Strauss, & Giroux, 1985).

*Assata*, Assata Shakur, (Lawrence Hill Books, 1985).

*The Color Purple*, Alice Walker, (Harcourt Brace, 1982).

*Billy*, Albert French, (Viking Penguin, 1995).

*Their Eyes Were Watching God*, Zora Neale Hurston, (Harper Perennial, 1990).

## CHANGING DIETS, CHANGING LIFESTYLES

*Healing With Whole Foods*, Paul Pitchford. Revised edition. (North Atlantic Books, 1996).

*Vibrational Medicine: New Choices for Healing Ourselves*, Richard Gerber, M.D. Revised edition. (Bear & Co., 1996).

*Planetary Herbology*, Dr. Michael Tierra, (Lotus Press, 1988).

*The Yoga of Herbs: An Ayurvedic Guide to Herbal Medicine*, Dr. David Frawley & Dr. Vasant Lad, (Lotus Press, 1986).

*Bach Flower Therapy: Theory and Practice*, Mechthild Scheffer, (Healing Arts Press, 1988).

*Manual of Homeopathic Materia Medica*, William Boericke, M.D., (Boericke & Tafel, 1927).

*Clean & Green: Complete Guide to Nontoxic and Environmentally Safe Housekeeping*, Annie Berthold-Bond, (Ceres Press, 1990).

*The McDougall Plan*, Dr. John McDougall, (New Century, 1985).

*Fresh from a Vegetarian Kitchen: 450 Delicious Recipes*, Meredith McCarty, (St. Martin's Press, 1995).

*The Nourishment for Life Cookbook*, Rachel & Don Matesz, (1998).

*Dr. Pitcairn's Complete Guide to Natural Health for Dogs and Cats*, Richard Pitcairn, D.V.M., & Susan Pitcairn, (Rodale, 1995).

**Most of the books recommended for Further Reading in the NATURE AND ANIMALS & CHANGING DIETS, CHANGING LIFESTYLES sections are available for purchase from I.D.E.A.**

# NOTES

1. H.L. Edlin, *England's Forests*, (London: Faber and Faber, 1958), 17-21; Edlin, *Forestry and Woodland Life*, (London: Batsford, 1947), 73-80.
2. Roderick Nash, *The Wilderness and the American Mind*, (New Haven/London: Yale University Press, 1967), 27.
3. *Ibid.*, 24.
4. Aphra Behn, *Oroonoko, or, The Royal Slave*, (London: Will. Canning, 1688). Reprint, (New York: W.W. Norton, 1973), 66.
5. James Baldwin, "An Open Letter to My Sister, Angela Y. Davis," in *If They Come In the Morning: Voices of Resistance*, (New American Library, 1971), 20-21.
6. Charles Darwin, *The Descent of Man*, (London: J. Murray, 1871), 105.
7. *Ibid.*, 35.
8. Michel Eyquem de Montaigne, "Apology for Raimond Sebond," *Essays*, (1580-8); cited in John Gross, *The Oxford Book of Aphorisms*, (New York: Oxford University Press, 1987), 353.
9. Lichtenberg, *Aphorisms*, 1764-99; cited in John Gross, *Aphorisms*, 6.
10. *Ibid.*, 4.
11. In *The Descent of Man*, Charles Darwin lists, in addition to those mentioned in the text of this book, several attributes claimed to belong to humans alone. They include: "that man alone is capable of progressive improvement; that he alone makes use of... fire, domesticates other animals, [or] possesses property...; that no other animal is self-conscious, comprehends itself, has the power of abstraction, or possesses general ideas; that man alone has a sense of beauty, is liable to caprice, has the feeling of gratitude, mystery, etc.; believes in God, or is endowed with a conscience." Darwin ably refutes those he merits as the most important of these points. (*Descent of Man*, 49-69.)
12. Perry Phillips, *Ten Common Arguments Against Animal Rights Refuted*, First Edition, (Seattle: People For Animals Press, 1986), 2.
13. Michel Eyquem de Montaigne, "Apology for Raimond Sebond," *Essays*, (1580-8); D.M. Frame (trans.), *The Complete Essays of Montaigne*, (Garden City: Anchor Books, 1960), 130-131.
14. René Descartes, *Discours de la méthode*, 5; A. Bridoux, ed., *Oeuvres et lettres de Descartes*, (Dijon: Gallimard, 1953), 165-166. Cited in M. Cartmill, *A View to a Death in the Morning*, (Cambridge: Harvard

University Press, 1993), 95.

15. *Ibid.*, 95.

16. Jeffrey Moussaieff Masson, *When Elephants Weep: The Emotional Lives of Animals,* (New York: Delacorte Press, 1995), 229. This book explores the great depth and breadth of animals' experiences.

17. Cited in The Princeton Language Institute, *21st Century Dictionary of Quotations,* (New York: Dell Publishing, 1993), 27.

18. Keith Thomas, *Man and the Natural World,* (New York: Pantheon, 1983), 44; citing Moryson from Day, *Day's Descent,* 213.

19. A.R. Wallace, 'Quarterly Review," April 1869, 392; cited in Darwin, *Descent of Man,* 137.

20. Sterling A. Brown, "Negro Character as Seen by White Authors," in *Dark Symphony: Negro Literature in America,* (New York: The Free Press, 1968), 155-156.

21. *Ibid.*, 156.

22. *Ibid.*, 157.

23. *Ibid.*, 156.

24. Saint Augustine of Hippo, *On Original Sin*; W.J. Oates, ed., *Basic Writings of Saint Augustine,* vol. 1, (New York: Modern Library, 1948), 652.

25. Philip P. Hallie, *Cruelty,* (Middletown, CT: Wesleyan University Press, 1982), 107-108.

26. Solomon Northrup, "Picking Cotton . . .", cited in Hallie, *Cruelty,* 116.

27. It is important to keep in mind that most of the Africans who eventually became slaves in America were initially kidnapped by other blacks. As such, the slave trade was not a simple case of white oppression of black, but of the powerful preying upon the weak.

28. Sir Harry H. Johnston, *The Negro in the New World,* (London: Methuen and Co., 1910), 376.

29. Report from Richmond, VA, *The New York Tribune,* 3 March 1853. Cited in A.C. Carey, *Slave Trade—Domestic and Foreign: Why it exists and how it may be extinguished,* 1853.

30. This figure includes adults and infants killed in the process of capture, as well as infants who die en route to their overseas destination.

31. J. Howard Moore, from *The Universal Kinship,* cited in Jon Wynne Tyson, *The Extended Circle: A Dictionary of Humane Thought,* (Sussex, England: Centaur Press, Ltd., 1985), 215.

32. G. Jensen and C. Tolman, "Mother-infant relationship in the monkey, *Macaca nemestrina*: The effect of brief separation and mother-infant specificity," *J. Comp. Physiol. Psychol.,* 1962, 55: 132-133.

33. Cited in J. Duffy, *Portuguese Africa*, (Cambridge: Harvard University Press, 1959), 104.
34. Cited in C.W. Hume, "Blind Spots," originally published in *Everybody's Weekly*, 10 August 1946; from reprint in expanded form, (London: UFAW, 5 November 1946), 3.
35. Cited in Daniel P. Mannix and Malcolm Cowley, *Black Cargoes: A History of the Atlantic Slave Trade, 1518-1865*, (New York: Viking Press, 1962), 106.
36. *Ibid.*, 108.
37. *Ibid.*, 105.
38. *Ibid.*, 150.
39. *Ibid.*, 106.
40. Cited in *ibid.*, 126.
41. Halal (Moslem) ritual slaughter requires that animals be fully conscious during the kill, a requirement shared with Kosher ritual slaughter. Under proscribed Halal slaughter laws, however, there is no code requiring sharpening the knife between each animal, nor that the kill be completed in one stroke of the knife. Frequently, an animal receives many cuts on its neck with a dull knife before blood-loss ends its life. While Kosher slaughter requires that only one knife-stroke is made, animals still hang suspended while bleeding to death.
42. When interstate transportation of animals is involved, it is mandatory—under The Livestock Transportation Act of 1906—that animals be fed, watered, and let out of the transport vehicles every 28 hours. Under the present system, however, this protective legislation is virtually unenforceable—and thus unenforced.
43. Cited by Therese Becker in M. Morgan and P. Fischer, eds., *Cracks in the Ark: Poems About Animals*, (Jonesboro: Writers for Animal Rights, 1982), 6.
44. John Howard Griffin, *Black Like Me*, (Boston: Houghton-Mifflin, 1961), 99-102.
45. From a personal interview with a U.S. Fish and Wildlife Service Environmental Contaminants Specialist, 18 August 1995.
46. While no ban exists on the use of lead shot for either upland game-hunting or trap & skeet shooting, hunting- and shooting-caused environmental lead contamination continues.
47. Each state's Fish and Wildlife Service distributes hunting licenses, and collects data on the number of *reported* kills. This figure, estimated by a New York State Fish and Wildlife Service agent, is based

on the number of hunting licenses issued, minus those restricted to small game. The figure was further reduced, for the sake of accuracy, to allow both for hunters pursuing other large animals in deer ranges, and for states in which deer hunting is not as common.

48. Christine Ammer, *It's Raining Cats & Dogs... and Other Beastly Expressions*, (New York: Paragon House, 1989), 124-125.

49. Johnston, *Negro in the New World*, 377-378.

50. A recent amendment to the Marine Mammal Protection Act permits importing the bodies of slaughtered polar bears into the United States.

51. Michelle Russell, "Slave Codes and Liner Notes," in *Heresies #10: Women and Music*.

52. Joseph Wood Krutch, *The Great Chain of Life*, (Boston: Houghton Mifflin, 1956), 147-148. Cited in M. Cartmill, *View to a Death*, 228. Cartmill notes that the last sentence of Krutch's comment, 'I am the Spirit that Denies,' "identifies the hunter as a literally satanic figure by putting into his mouth the words of Goethe's Mephistopheles— 'Ich bin der Geist, der stets verneint'."

53. This figure is an estimate; an exact figure is impossible to obtain, because only animals procured from across State lines need be reported to the Federal Government. In the U.S., at least 19 million additional animals die each year in classroom dissection.

54. This figure from the British Union for the Abolition of Vivisection.

55. See James H. Jones, *Bad Blood*, (London: The Free Press, 1981).

56. Richard Wright, "The Man Who Went to Chicago," in W. Adams, ed., *Afro-American Authors*, (Boston: Houghton-Mifflin, 1972), 49.

57. Western medicine is excellent for emergency response to traumatic injury and the acute crises of ignored chronic conditions, and some of its technologies provide for accurate diagnoses of acute conditions. An intelligent approach to medicine would utilize the strengths of both systems: Western for emergency response and physical repair to injured bones and tissues; holistic medicine for prevention and healing. Even within the Western medical paradigm, research involving animals as experimental subjects is unnecessary; many books and journals are available on non-animal research methodologies.

58. The *Further Reading* section of this book (under "Changing Diets, Changing Lifestyles") suggests a number of excellent titles on preventative medicine, alternative health care, and food as medicine.

59. Aristotle, *Politics*, 1.5.

60. Brown, *Negro Character*, 142.

61. John P. Kennedy, *Swallow Barn*, (Carey and Lea, 1832), cited in Brown, "Negro Character," 142.
62. Philip Slater, *The Pursuit of Loneliness: American Culture at the Breaking Point*, (Boston: Beacon Press, 1970), 21-22.
63. Phillips Verner Bradford & Harvey Blume, *Ota Benga*, (New York: St. Martin's, 1992), 168-190. Ten years after his release from the zoo, and unable to afford passage back to Africa, Ota Benga committed suicide.
64. Hallie, *Cruelty*, 102.
65. Cited in Susan Griffin, *Woman and Nature*, (New York: Harper & Row, 1978), 69.
66. Charles Westley Hume, *The Status of Animals in the Christian Religion*, (London: Universities Federation for Animal Welfare, 1956).
67. The Bible, (*author's synthesis of several translations*), Exodus 20:17.
68. *Ibid.*, Exodus 21:29.
69. *Ibid.*, Exodus 21:23-25.
70. Many of the biblical passages recognizing and approving of slavery were cited by Charles Pellegrino in his fascinating book, *Return to Sodom and Gomorrah*, (New York: Random House, 1994), 241-244.
71. The Bible, Exodus 21:4.
72. *Ibid.*, Exodus 21:5-6.
73. *Ibid.*, Numbers 21:34-35.
74. *Ibid.*, Numbers 31:9-18.
75. *Ibid.*, Deuteronomy 3:6-7.
76. Alan Moorehead, *Darwin and the Beagle*, (New York: Penguin Books, 1971), 99.
77. Cited in *ibid.*, 50.
78. Coral Lansbury, *The Old Brown Dog: Women, Workers, and Vivisection in Edwardian England*, (Madison: University of Wisconsin, 1985), 32.
79. Susan Griffin, *Pornography and Silence*, (New York: Harper & Row, 1981), 169-170.
80. Cited in Nash, *Wilderness and the American Mind*, 29.
81. *Ibid.*, 29.
82. Robert Wernick, "Speaking Out: Let's Spoil the Wilderness," *Saturday Evening Post*, 238 (6 Nov. 1965), 12. Cited in Nash, *Wilderness and the American Mind*, 27.
83. Lansbury, *Old Brown Dog*, 119-120.
84. *Ibid.*, 91.
85. *Ibid.*, 119.
86. *The New York Times*, 23 December 1986, A1; 21 December 1986, A1.

# ACKNOWLEDGMENTS

The Author and MIRROR BOOKS/I.D.E.A. would like to gratefully acknowledge the support of the following individuals, foundations, and corporations who greatly assisted in the creation of this book:

Andrew Merson and Command Web Offset for the beautiful printing of the book; Ron Hans, Lars-Gunnar Larrson, Jakob Jonnson, Lisa Smedman, Jeff Mendelsohn, and Stora, for their immeasurable help with the paper on which this book is printed; Rich Campisi and Graphic Lab for image scanning and production assistance; Robert Plant and Superior Printing Ink Company for their special attention to the inks used; Alice Walker for the foreword; Gordon Parks for the words he first wrote for the last edition; Maria Coughlin and Editorial Services for the index; Brian Adams and Soho Black & White for photographic services; The Ahimsa Foundation, The Puffin Foundation, NALITH, Syed Rizvi, Eileen Weintraub, and many members of I.D.E.A. for their support; Ben Ko, Dan Franck, and Heather Wood for their incomparable help; Jill Siegel, Martin Rowe, Mark Robert, Jim and Paul Drougas, David Siegel, Mike Markarian, Todd Patterson, Dean Smith, Charles Patterson, David Leslie, Margaret Murray, I.D.E.A. interns and other volunteers for their assistance; Muriel and Victor Polikoff, and Jody Wilkie at Christie's, for their help with Wedgwood history. And to those who could not be thanked in name here: it's to you that this book is dedicated.

The publisher has made every effort to credit the appropriate sources for the materials contained in this book. Any omissions are unintentional. Credits and/or permissions for illustrations are acknowledged as follows:

Marjorie Spiegel, cover photo; The Bettman Archive, 6 (top image), 36, 42 (bottom image), 81 (top), 97; The New York Historical Society, 6 (bottom); Wide World Photos, 28; The Mansell Collection, 29, 53 (top), 78 (slave posters), 100; James B. Mason, 47, 56; *The Age*, Melbourne, 51; USDA, 53 (bottom); Environmental Investigation Agency, 54; Wayland Picture Archive, 55; *The Seattle Times*, 63; Center for Disease Control, Atlanta, 69; BUAV, 81 (bottom), 101.

# INDEX

S

T

V

W

Z

125

# ABOUT THE AUTHOR

MARJORIE SPIEGEL is a documentary photographer and the author of several books. Her fields of study include biology, philosophy, environmental studies, history, nutrition, and medicine. In 1989, she founded I.D.E.A., THE INSTITUTE FOR THE DEVELOPMENT OF EARTH AWARENESS, a nonprofit educational organization whose mission synthesizes three areas of concern: environmental, human, and animal issues. Ms. Spiegel believes that because the world is a complex web which inseparably links together the earth, humans, and other animals, efforts to effect positive change—whether on an individual or global level—must also reflect this interconnectedness, and that less unified efforts by organizations addressing only single issues can not succeed at effectively stemming the threats to personal and planetary survival which we presently face. Marjorie Spiegel currently serves as I.D.E.A.'s Executive Director. The organization is more fully described on the following pages.

# ABOUT THIS BOOK

This Revised and Expanded Edition of *The Dreaded Comparison* was published by MIRROR BOOKS, the nonprofit publishing division of I.D.E.A., THE INSTITUTE FOR THE DEVELOPMENT OF EARTH AWARENESS.

*The Dreaded Comparison* was printed by Command Web Offset, in Secaucus, New Jersey. It was printed with vegetable-oil-based inks supplied by Superior Printing Ink Company. The black ink used has the added distinction of being recycled—a process in which unused inks are returned to the manufacturer and reformulated rather than being discarded.

The book was printed on *Cyclus* 100% post-consumer recycled paper, which is manufactured by Stora. Unlike virtually all other commercial book papers, *Cyclus* is bleached without chlorine, so it does not create dioxin—a highly toxic by-product of chlorine-bleaching. As defined by European standards, "100% post-consumer recycled" means that *Cyclus* is made entirely from paper that was pulled out of the consumer waste-stream, reclaimed from end-users, and from manufactured items that weren't sold. Unlike most other papers termed "recycled," *Cyclus* does not contain any virgin wood-pulp, nor mill scraps from virgin paper production.

We at I.D.E.A./MIRROR BOOKS are proud to be the first publisher in North America to produce a book in the most environmentally-sustainable manner possible today. We would like to encourage other publishers to join us in our commitment to responsible, sustainable publishing. For more information about ecologically-sound materials and publishing, please feel free to contact us.

All of the proceeds from the sale of this book benefit the educational projects and programs of I.D.E.A.

# ABOUT I.D.E.A.

 THE INSTITUTE FOR THE DEVELOPMENT OF EARTH AWARENESS (I.D.E.A.) is an all-volunteer, 501(c)(3) nonprofit organization founded in 1989 by author/photographer MARJORIE SPIEGEL. In its educational work, I.D.E.A. addresses the causes—rather than the symptoms—of the problems currently facing the earth and its inhabitants. I.D.E.A.'s mission is to help our society reestablish a harmonious relationship with the natural world. To accomplish this, we endeavor to help people understand the cultural, behavioral, and spiritual roots of our relationship with nature. We provide in-depth information about the earth's ecology, and how to live and work with the earth instead of in opposition to it. We strive to further an awareness of the inexorable link between humans and the environment. I.D.E.A. believes this integrated approach to education is essential to helping us understand the complexity of our world, so that we may learn to live in unity with the planet and each other.

I.D.E.A. utilizes the arts in its work towards a sustainable future. We are involved in a wide range of projects, including multi-media educational projects and campaigns; investigative and documental research; the production of special musical and cultural events; MIRROR BOOKS, our book publishing and distribution division; THE ADOPT-A-LIBRARY PROGRAM; THE KEY & CASTLE PROJECT, directed by I.D.E.A.'s Vice President ANTON ERLACHER, developing and implementing bio-sustainable building techniques; prevention of toxins in the home and workplace; nutrition & alternative medicine information resources; land and wildlife preserves; and habitat revitalization. An integral part of all of I.D.E.A.'s projects is education.